Ask Me About My Jesus

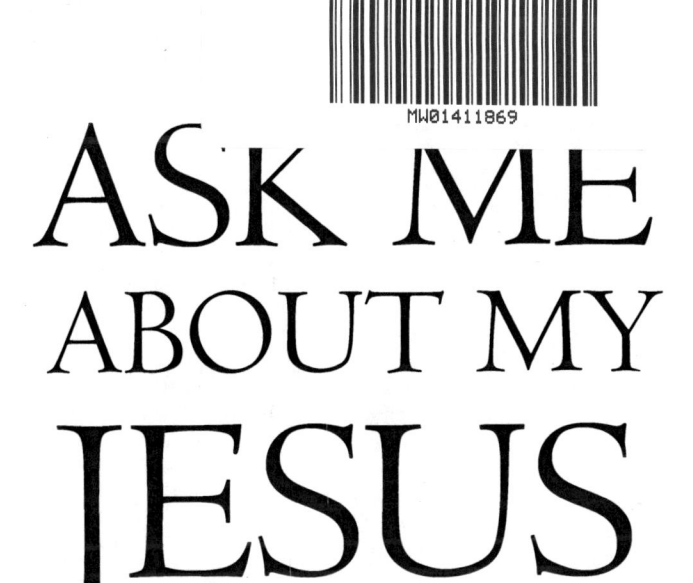

90 DAYS TO A CLOSER WALK WITH JESUS

LuAnn Gerig Fulton

5 Fold Media
Visit us at www.5foldmedia.com

Ask Me about My Jesus: 90 Days to a Closer Walk with Jesus
Copyright 2017 by LuAnn Gerig Fulton
Published by 5 Fold Media, LLC
www.5foldmedia.com

All rights reserved. No part of this book may be reproduced, stored in a retrieval system, or transmitted in any form or by any means-electronic, mechanical, photocopy, recording, or otherwise-without prior written permission of the copyright owner. The views and opinions expressed from the writer are not necessarily those of 5 Fold Media, LLC. Additional emphasis in Scripture quotations are author's own.

All Scripture quotations are taken from *Holy Bible,* New Living Translation, copyright © 1996, 2004, 2015 by Tyndale House Foundation. Used by permission of Tyndale House Publishers Inc., Carol Stream, Illinois 60188. All rights reserved.

ISBN: 978-1-942056-53-9

Library of Congress Control Number: 2017953326

Printed in the USA.

This book is dedicated to my grandchildren.

I was told for many years that being a Grandma was something wonderful, and even though I knew that was probably true, there was no way I could really understand it until I became one. As each of you entered the world, my heart expanded to hold more love than I ever imagined was possible. As I looked into your eyes, I vowed to do all I could do to be the grandma that Jesus would want me to be.

I want each of you to know that I will always have time for you. Remember that Grandma loves you more than you will ever know and that spending time with you is a blessing. I want to have fun with you, explore with you, and laugh with you. I want to listen to your funny stories and play make-believe. I want to hold you, read to you, and kiss your boo-boos. And there will be times when I will just want to "be" with you, without having to do anything at all.

I will not be successful as a grandma though, if all you remember about me is that I was someone with whom you had fun. More importantly, I want you to be able to remember me as a Grandma who loved her Jesus with all her heart. When you are with me, I want you to see Jesus. When I talk with you, I want you to hear words from Jesus. When we explore this great big world together, I want you to find Jesus. When I hold you close to me, I want you to feel Jesus in a special way.

There is nothing more in this world that I want for you than to love my Jesus with all your heart. He will never leave you or disappoint you. He gave everything so that you can walk with Him with every step, every day, and someday spend eternity with Him.

Unfortunately, I'm not going to be a perfect Grandma, but I hope my love for you will outshine my imperfections. My prayer is that as we do life together, each of us will learn and grow from each other and become better Christ-followers as a result of our relationship.

When you read this book, I want it to remind you of just how much I love my Jesus and how much I love you. You are truly a blessing to me.

Love and lots of kisses,

Grandma

Contents

	Preface	9
DAY 1	My Story, My Jesus	13
DAY 2	His Love	15
DAY 3	Jesus, Our Friend	18
DAY 4	Ready and Willing	21
DAY 5	Miracle Moments I	24
DAY 6	Miracle Moments II	26
DAY 7	Miracle Moments III	29
DAY 8	A Look Within	32
DAY 9	In the Meantime…	34
DAY 10	Get Up!	37
DAY 11	Feeling Loved	40
DAY 12	Is The Sky Falling?	42
DAY 13	An Act Of Kindness	44
DAY 14	In the Eyes of My Beholders	47
DAY 15	A Work in Progress	49
DAY 16	Chill Pill	52
DAY 17	A Beach Experience I	55
DAY 18	A Beach Experience II	57
DAY 19	A Beach Experience III	59
DAY 20	A Beach Experience IV	61
DAY 21	A Beach Experience V	63
DAY 22	Staying Connected	66
DAY 23	A New Beginning	69

DAY 24	Are You Willing To Tinkle?	71
DAY 25	Best-Laid Plans	73
DAY 26	Confessions From a Cheapskate	76
DAY 27	A "Shredding Experience"	78
DAY 28	Be Still	80
DAY 29	Connecting to the Power…	82
DAY 30	CPR	84
DAY 31	Created in His Image	86
DAY 32	Faith in Action	89
DAY 33	God's To-Do List	91
DAY 34	The Rest of the Story	93
DAY 35	Life is Short	95
DAY 36	He Knew, But He Still Loved	98
DAY 37	Service or Serve-Us?	101
DAY 38	How Bad Is Your Bark?	103
DAY 39	If Only…	105
DAY 40	Italian Broccoli	107
DAY 41	Just Not Feeling It…	109
DAY 42	Life Stinks	111
DAY 43	Light Bulb Moments	113
DAY 44	Living Life As A Worrywart	116
DAY 45	Loving Forever	118
DAY 46	Moving Mountains	120
DAY 47	Pruning Petunias	122
DAY 48	Pride and My Big Mouth	124
DAY 49	Priorities	127
DAY 50	So Big!	129

DAY 51	Resolutions	131
DAY 52	The Choice Is Yours to Make	134
DAY 53	The "Compare Game"	136
DAY 54	Time To Be Fruitful	138
DAY 55	To Be or Not to Be…Selfish	140
DAY 56	The Test	142
DAY 57	Transparency	144
DAY 58	The Swing Set	147
DAY 59	Wandering Minds	149
DAY 60	Save a Seat For Me	151
DAY 61	The Oven	153
DAY 62	Let's Do This!	155
DAY 63	What Will I Leave Behind?	157
DAY 64	Memories	160
DAY 65	Lord, Help Me	162
DAY 66	Not Once!	165
DAY 67	Because I Said So	167
DAY 68	Imposing Our Way	170
DAY 69	At His Feet	173
DAY 70	Being Prepared	175
DAY 71	Perspectives	177
DAY 72	Thinking Like Jesus	180
DAY 73	Memories to Ponder	182
DAY 74	The Small "Talk Box"	184
DAY 75	Rest…Now?	186
DAY 76	Worth The Cost	189
DAY 77	Imperfect People	192

DAY 78	Newborns	196
DAY 79	Hand in Hand	198
DAY 80	Charging Station	200
DAY 81	He's Watching Me	202
DAY 82	Choosing To Laugh	204
DAY 83	Change Begins at Home	206
DAY 84	Blessed and Doubly Blessed	209
DAY 85	Off The Grid	212
DAY 86	Life Happens	214
DAY 87	'Tis The Season	216
DAY 88	Life's Videos	218
DAY 89	Taming My Unibrow	221
DAY 90	A Glimpse Of Heaven	223

Preface

I grew up in a fishbowl. Well, not literally. I did own quite a few goldfish over the years, but none of their habitats were large enough for me to join them. But I often felt like I understood exactly how those fish felt.

The reason for this is that I'm a PK, a preacher's kid. Not only am I a PK, I'm also a PG, preacher's grandchild, and a PN, preacher's niece. In my dad's family, you were either a preacher, married to a preacher, or a missionary in Africa. In my mom's family, all three girls married ministers. One of the positives of this was that we never had to worry at a family gathering whether there would be anyone to say the blessing for the meal.

Have you ever walked up to an aquarium and just stood and stared at every move the fish made? A PK often feels like those fish. People walking by, taking notes of every move you make, and then cataloging that information to use at a later date. I don't think most people did this to make me and my siblings feel "different"; it was just the way it was.

A pastor's family is always on display. The kids are always being watched to make sure that their behavior is worthy of the family to which they were born, and the parents are being watched to make sure their children are angelic. We were expected to be perfect: always happy and displaying the joy of the Lord.

In the era that I grew up, people just didn't look at the pastor's family as being "normal" with daily stresses and problems like everyone else. I will never forget the time my parents were painting a room in our home. The doorbell rang, my dad answered it, and a member of our congregation stood there with his mouth hanging open. He couldn't believe that my dad wasn't wearing a shirt and tie. I guess he thought that ministers had a suit specifically for painting.

I also remember going to school one day upset because I had had an argument with my parents that morning. A friend of mine was mortified. She said, "I didn't think your family ever argued because your dad is a minister." I tried to explain to her that we were a normal family whose dad just happened to be a pastor, but I don't think she ever understood.

Of course, there were also positives to being a PK. In one of the churches, a member of our congregation owned an ice cream company and always made sure our freezer was full with delectable delights. Then there was the time that Corrie ten Boom came to our church to speak. Since I was the PK, I had the honor and privilege of meeting her and shaking her hand. She was a woman of amazing grace who just oozed God's love to everyone she met.

My dad had amazing pastorates and was well known in the communities in which we lived, so I was never really known as LuAnn Gerig, I was always referred to as Rev. Gerig's daughter. Once that was said, the connection was made and I knew to behave.

As an adult, I realized that I also took advantage of that connection. It was easy to hide behind the title of being Rev. Gerig's daughter. As a result, I really didn't have to claim my own relationship with the Lord. I accepted Christ at the ripe old age of six, but growing up everyone just assumed that because I was a PK, my walk with the Lord was where it should be. In some ways, I did too. I had the false presumption that because I came from a long line of ministers, I automatically had an "in," and their walk would become mine. I was a good kid, rarely doing anything that wouldn't have been acceptable, but I didn't have the close relationship that I should have had with my Jesus.

The ironic part of my story is that I went from living in a fishbowl to marrying a "fishman." The man I fell in love with at the age of twenty was a caterer, doing fish frys for non-profit and civic organizations. Dan was also well known because of his business, so I traded the label of Rev. Gerig's daughter to Mrs. Fish Fry. Fortunately, Dan had a strong relationship with Jesus, but unfortunately, that just gave me another person to hide behind. I figured he could be the spiritual leader in our home and I would be the wife and eventual mother to our three children.

That seemed to work until I found myself overwhelmed with raising those three children born in a span of four-and-a-half years. Due to Dan's hectic schedule, I was often left at home with the kids by myself. I also suffered from numerous health issues, so finding the energy to get through each day with three healthy, active children left me feeling exhausted mentally, physically, and spiritually.

Looking back, I realize that this time in my life would probably have been much easier if I had made it a priority to develop my own relationship with the Lord. I remember often breaking down in tears, just feeling like my life didn't have much purpose. Of course, raising children is one of the most difficult, challenging and rewarding opportunities a person will ever have, but sadly, I didn't always see it that way.

I remember the day when I finally gave everything I had over to the Lord. I told Him that I realized I couldn't do this on my own and that I would do whatever it took to be the child that He deserved. I had no idea where this decision would take me or what would be asked of me, but I was finally ready to walk through the doors that He opened.

It has been quite a journey since that day, and I'm now excited when people ask me about *my* Jesus; not my father's Jesus, or my husband's, or anyone else's. Now I know that my relationship with the Lord is *my* responsibility and *my* privilege. I won't enter through the gates of heaven some day because of my godly heritage, but because I have made the choice to have the King of Kings and Lord of Lords in the center of *my* life.

In these devotionals, I share with you glimpses of my walk with Him and how He has been molding and shaping me. My prayer is that my willingness to be open and transparent with you will help you desire to have a personal relationship with our Lord Jesus Christ, a relationship that is your very own, not one that is from the shirttail of another.

DAY 1

My Story, My Jesus

So never be ashamed to tell others about our Lord. And don't be ashamed of me, either, even though I'm in prison for him. With the strength God gives you, be ready to suffer with me for the sake of the Good News (2 Timothy 1:8).

On October 3rd, 1981, a beautiful fall day, I married my soul mate, Dan. At the time, I thought that I loved him as much as I could ever love someone, but over the years I have discovered that my love then was probably based more on infatuation than true love. The good times and the difficult times that we have since faced have served to deepen my love for him in ways I never could have imagined.

If you ever approach me and ask me about Dan, make sure you have time to listen. Because when I am asked about him, I'm never at a loss for words. I know that I could hold you hostage for a very long time, telling you how much he means to me. Don't misunderstand me; he isn't perfect, but that is a good thing! If he was, he wouldn't want to be married to me. We both have our strengths and our weaknesses, but together with Christ at the helm, our lives become complete.

Furthermore, if you approach me and ask me about our children, Erica, Megan, and Adam, you'd best take a seat. We have been blessed with the three greatest kids in the world as well as a phenomenal son-in-law, John, and daughter–in-law, Katie. Why, I could keep you enthralled for hours just listing time after time that they have each made us so very proud. Every time I think that I just couldn't love them anymore than I do, I am proven wrong and I feel my love for them soar to new heights.

Then there are my grandchildren, Elias, Ezekiel, and Emma. Not only would I have story after story to share with you as to how amazing and gifted they are, I would also have a photo album to show you. There are just no words to describe how proud this grandma is of her adorable, precious grandchildren.

The funny thing is that if you do ask me about my family, it won't matter whether I know you well or not. You could be someone that I've known for years, or you could be a complete stranger. In either situation, you are bound to get an earful because I love sharing stories about those I dearly love. I won't feel embarrassed to share or worried that I might make a fool of myself either. I surely won't keep quiet, thinking someone else will come along and tell you about my family so that I don't have to do it. They mean too much to me to leave it to someone else.

And now, because of the journey I have been on, I feel the same way about my Jesus. I used to fear that I would look like a "Jesus freak" if I spoke too much about Him. I didn't want to step on anyone's toes by imposing my beliefs on others, especially if I didn't know them well. I think I often thought that the Lord would send someone else to share about Him so I wouldn't have to do it. But I have realized that I can't wait for someone else to tell you or anyone else about Jesus. He expects me to be willing and ready to share the good news every chance I get!

What is your story? Do you find yourself talking to others more about your family than about your Jesus? Are you excited when others ask you about your Savior, or do you hope they leave you alone and ask someone else? I admit it; it can be scary. But I will let you in on a little secret as we begin these days of study together. There are many people in our world today who are longing to hear your story. They are yearning to know that the answer to their struggles can be found in your Jesus. You just have to be willing to tell them.

My Jesus Prayer

Jesus, thank You so much for wanting a personal relationship with me. Please teach me Your ways during these next ninety days, so we will be drawn closer together. As I grow in You, give me the courage to let others know how much You mean to me.

DAY 2

His Love

For this is how God loved the world: He gave his one and only Son, so that everyone who believes in him will not perish but have eternal life (John 3:16).

When I was in elementary school, I used to go over to my girlfriend's home and we would play church. Of course, because my dad was a minister, I always got to be the preacher. And every time I stood before my audience of one, I preached about John 3:16. I especially liked the part where it said that He gave His one and only Son, because at that point I would always pound my fist on the makeshift podium and say, "He didn't have five sons to choose from! He only had one!" Even at a young age, this fact made an impression on me.

As an adult, this verse still impacts me every time I read it. The facts are still the same. God was willing to sacrifice His one and only Son for me, even with all of my faults and failures, so that I could have eternal life. Christ was willing to be nailed to a cross so that He could be my Savior, my Redeemer.

Honestly, I have trouble comprehending this kind of love. I've tried to liken it to the love that I have for my family because I would give my life for Dan and for my children. But this still isn't a fair comparison, because I know that my family loves me. Christ was willing to endure a horrific crucifixion so that He could be the Savior for the world: everyone—whether they love Him in return or not. His love for us never wavers; it is constant. We are the ones who have the choice whether or not to accept it.

For Christ to be my Savior He had to believe that I was worth saving. In turn, if I am to act and react like Him, I need to view each person I meet as someone who is worth saving. Sometimes I struggle with that concept because there are people I meet who, at first glance, don't come up to my "standards." My critical spirit raises its ugly head and I make the rash decision that just because they may not look or act like me, they aren't worth my time or effort. I can usually come up with a long list of excuses as to why I shouldn't waste my time telling them about my Jesus. I even justify my actions by saying a quick prayer, asking the Lord to send someone else who is more like them to make sure they know there is a Savior who gave His life for them.

I remember meeting a woman one day. My initial thought was, *Now there is a hard woman who surely doesn't know the Lord.* Unfortunately my thoughts didn't come out of concern for her, they came from being judgmental. I began talking to her and it wasn't long until she was telling me how much her Jesus meant to her and the different Bible studies that she attended. I felt so ashamed of myself. I had let a person's outer appearance skew my thoughts into thinking things about them that were far from the truth. As I had the privilege of getting to know her, I soon realized what a sweet, genuine spirit she had, and how her walk with the Lord was an example to me as to how I should be living.

What a tragedy that I would act this way, because there are no "standards" when it comes to whom Christ came to save! I am no better or worse than anyone else, and He doesn't rank us according to our looks or behavior. There is nothing in my life or in yours that keeps Christ from loving us; He loves us right where we are, but has wonderful plans for us in the future.

Don't ever forget that this verse in John doesn't read, "For this is how God loved the world: He gave his one and only Son, so that everyone *(unless you have done drugs, or had an abortion, or had an affair, or are divorced, or have been an abusive parent or spouse, or have been raped or abused)* who believes in him will not perish but have eternal life." His love, His forgiveness, His offer of eternal life is for everyone who believes.

Whatever your past, whatever your looks, whatever your beliefs, I want to make sure you know that God sent His only Son to die for you so that He could become your Savior. He's my Savior and I want to make sure that He is yours too!

LUANN GERIG FULTON

My Jesus Prayer

Jesus, help me to see others and myself through Your eyes, remembering that You love all of us equally. Forgive me for dwelling on the faults of others and on the transgressions of my past, because I know Your forgiveness wipes me clean and new!

DAY 3
Jesus, Our Friend

And so it happened just as the Scriptures say: "Abraham believed God, and God counted him as righteous because of his faith." He was even called the friend of God (James 2:23).

I have different kinds of friends in my life. I have people who I know that I rarely see, but I would still introduce them to you as my friend. There are other people in my life that I see on a much more regular basis, maybe at church every Sunday or throughout the week, who I would also consider my friends. All of these individuals have a special place in my life and I feel blessed to know them.

But if I honestly look at my relationships with most of these people, I really don't *know* them very well. I don't know all of their likes and dislikes, what their favorite foods are, what their favorite hobby is, or even what colors they like best. I don't have much of a clue as to what they desire in their hearts or what concerns keep them awake at night. If you asked me questions about them, I'm afraid I probably wouldn't know very many of the answers. The truth is that I know them, but I really don't *know* them.

However, there are a few people in my life (beside my family) that I would also introduce to you as my friends and I think I would do quite well if you inquired more closely about them. I do really *know* them. I've spent considerable time with them, through the good and through the bad, and I've learned what makes them tick. They have allowed me to be a part of their life on a much deeper level; and in turn, I have allowed them to be a part of mine.

One of those close friends is Mary. We first met in a working situation and it didn't take long to strike up a friendship. Now, many years later, I believe I can safely say that there is very little that I don't know about her and I am confident that there is very little that she doesn't know about me. Over time, our relationship has gone from being coworkers to being comrades, from being superficial to in-depth.

Do you know what I like best about Mary? She tells me what she thinks, even when she knows I probably don't want to hear it. She cares enough about me to let me unload on her and vent when I'm upset, but she never lets me stay there. One day I was in a frump. After encouraging me with uplifting words, she said, "Now grab those bootstraps, lady, put on that happy face, sing a song, and march on!" As you can imagine, I couldn't help but smile.

What is funny about her statement is that if she would have told me that when we first met, I probably would have been offended. I may have thought, *Who does she think she is, telling me to put on a happy face?* But because our friendship has been growing over many years, she knew exactly what words I needed to hear, and I knew that she cared enough about me to say them.

I have another friend who is even closer to me than Mary. He knows absolutely everything about me; I have no secrets with Him. His love for me never fluctuates or changes, and I never have to put on a front around Him.

We read in the Bible that this friend of mine, Jesus, was also Abraham's friend. Abraham was God's friend because he was willing to demonstrate his faith in God. He was willing to be obedient, and we are told to do the same. We need to be willing to do what He asks us to do and follow Him without hesitation. But it will be very difficult to do this unless we know Him intimately. Just as Mary and I know each other well because we have spent time together, we must also make it a priority to spend time with our friend Jesus and His heavenly Father.

Are you lonely today? Are you looking for a friend who will never leave you, never give up on you, never stop loving you? Look no further! Jesus is just waiting for you to accept Him as your Lord and Savior and then begin a friendship with Him that will last forever. Believe me when I say you will never regret making Him your very best friend.

My Jesus Prayer

Jesus, I want You to be my Lord and Savior and my very best friend. I want to spend time with You, so I can know You intimately. Thank You, Jesus for loving me right where I am today, but desiring so much more for me in the days ahead.

LUANN GERIG FULTON

DAY 4

Ready and Willing

Get rid of all bitterness, rage, anger, harsh words, and slander, as well as all types of evil behavior. Instead, be kind to each other, tenderhearted, forgiving one another, just as God through Christ has forgiven you (Ephesians 4:31-32).

Forgiveness. Not a word that is often easy to live out. To do so we usually have to display mercy and compassion and an attitude of reconciliation. It is an act that, as human beings, isn't always our first response to being hurt by another.

Our society doesn't encourage forgiveness very often either. Many times we are shown over and over that the response to pain is to get revenge any way that we can: Get even, make sure they hurt as bad as we do, and make them pay for what they have done to us.

However, if I spend time with my friend, Jesus, and learn from His teaching, I discover that there isn't any room in my life for revenge. I can't find even once in Scripture where I have a right to "set the score straight" with those who wound me. In fact, Matthew 5:44 tells me that instead of seeking revenge, I am to love my enemies and pray for those who have hurt me.

The event in the Bible that has had the greatest impact on me concerning forgiveness is the story of Jesus' crucifixion. I can't imagine what He must have felt like as He hung on that cross.

Think back to all that had transpired before that fateful day. Jesus had done nothing to deserve being treated in such a dreadful way. In His thirty-three years on this earth, he had:

- Healed Simon Peter's mother-in-law (Mark 1:29-31)
- Cleansed lepers (Luke 17:11-19)
- Restored a man's withered hand (Mark 3:1-6)

- Restored sight to blind men (Matthew 9:27-31 and other places)
- Raised a widow's son from the dead (Luke 7:11-17)
- Raised Lazarus from the dead (John 11:1-44)
- Calmed a storm on the Sea of Galilee (Mark 4:35-41)
- Fed 5000 people with five loaves of bread and two fish (Mark 6:32-44)
- Forgiven a prostitute (John 8:11)
- Healed a woman who had been crippled for eighteen years (Luke 13:10-17)

And that is just a miniscule list of what Jesus did for others. So wouldn't you think that when He was condemned to be crucified, there would have been throngs of people coming to His rescue? Shouldn't there have been hundreds, if not thousands, of His followers swarming His avengers, crying out that He had done nothing wrong, that He had only had their best interest in mind? Where were all these people when He was:

- Flogged with a lead-tipped whip (Mark 15:15)
- Stripped of His clothes (Matthew 27:28)
- Crowned with thorns (Matthew 27:29)
- Mocked and taunted (Matthew 27:29)
- Spit on and hit in the head with a stick (Matthew 27:30)
- Nailed to a cross (Matthew 27:35)
- Speared in His side (John 19:34)

I can't help but wonder if while Jesus was being led to Mt. Calvary, He periodically looked over His shoulder to see if those whose lives He had touched were following. Did He strain His ears to listen for their footsteps? Did He look from side to side, hoping someone was coming to protest? Surely they would all come to His rescue, surely they would come to His aid. I'm mean, if I would have been there, I would have spoken up, wouldn't I? Or would I have been like so many, who knew He was innocent and wrongly accused, but decided it was just too risky to get involved.

If that isn't hard enough to understand, we are then shocked in this story to read these words in Luke 23:34a, *"Jesus said, 'Father, forgive them, for they don't know what they are doing.'"* What? Are you kidding me?

Forgive them? That is preposterous! Why in the world should these heathens—these lowlifes—who were brutally killing an innocent man, be forgiven? They should be the ones who were crucified, not my Jesus. They didn't deserve to be forgiven. Why would Jesus say such a thing?

He said it because He loved them enough to forgive them. His concern for His accusers was greater than His concern for His own well-being and He knew there was a bigger picture to all of this. He realized that He had to look beyond His current situation, turning His eyes upward, knowing that what He was going through at that time was just for a moment. But what was to come would be for eternity.

Since Jesus is my forgive-or, I, in turn, need to be ready and willing to forgive those who have hurt me. Will it be easy? No. Will it cause me pain? Possibly. But I know I won't go through it alone. The One who suffered to a degree that I can't even comprehend, will be with me and will be my example to follow. I guess that is the least I can do for my Jesus.

My Jesus Prayer

Jesus, I can't imagine the pain and suffering You endured because of my sin. I didn't deserve it, but You freely gave Your all for me. Help me, Jesus, to extend the same kind of forgiveness You did to those who have wronged me, so they will see You in me.

DAY 5
Miracle Moments I

Now all glory to God, who is able, through his mighty power at work within us, to accomplish infinitely more than we might ask or think (Ephesians 3:20).

I often hear people question why we don't see amazing, mind-blowing miracles today like those witnessed in biblical times. We don't hear about someone feeding five-thousand people with one slab of ribs and a piece of cornbread. We don't come in contact with a person who was blind all their life, but had their sight restored by just a touch of a hand. And we surely don't turn on the evening news to hear that a neighbor of ours has been raised from the dead after taking his last breath four days prior. If events like this are happening, the general public is not getting the message.

Does that mean that God isn't capable of performing miracles in our day? Does it mean that those kind of miraculous events were only for biblical times and we just aren't blessed enough to experience them today? The answer to those questions is *no*. God *is* capable and He *is* still in the miracle-blessing business. I believe He wants nothing more than to shower us with His blessings and reveal His power that never runs out every single day.

The question then becomes, *why aren't we seeing the miracles that God is doing in our midst?* Unfortunately, I believe the answer might be because we aren't looking. We are so busy and have become so wrapped up in our day-to-day activities that we don't look for His hand in our lives. I'm afraid our faith is also not where it should be. As a result, we don't expect Him to work and it never occurs to us that He is able to do far more than we ever dreamed or hoped. I think we often forget how big our God is and that there is nothing He can't accomplish.

Miracles come in all sizes. They may be an event such as physical healing that occurs and lasts for a lifetime. Or they may be what I like to call "miracle moments": moments in time when something happens that can't be explained through medicine, wisdom, or coincidence; something that was the result of the hand of God.

The greatest, most powerful miracle moment occurred in my life in 2009 at the bedside of my ailing mother (I will tell more about that later). The time span was probably no more than three minutes from when the miracle began to when it ended, and if I hadn't been watching, I could have easily missed it. But those precious moments are something I will never forget. That day, God chose to show me His power as only He can do.

Be on the lookout today for "miracle moments" that God just might send your way. He is able to do far more than you can ever imagine and today just might be the day that you will be talking about for many years to come!

My Jesus Prayer

> *Jesus, it is so easy for me to become focused on myself. It is easy to forget to watch for Your mighty hand at work during my day. Keep me focused and always looking upward so I don't miss a miracle moment!*

DAY 6
Miracle Moments II

Jesus looked at them intently and said, "Humanly speaking, it is impossible. But with God everything is possible" (Matthew 19:26).

For you to better understand my miracle moment, it is necessary for me to give you some background. My mother had been ill for a very long time before I stood by her bedside that day in 2009. Ten years prior she had begun to show signs of dementia. We noticed her nerves were on edge and her thought processes were not clear. She became agitated easily, which was not at all like her normal personality.

My mom had always been a very sharp, talented person. She was very detail-orientated and could accomplish tasks that often baffled others. The last job that she had was being the final proofer for magazines. She often found errors that the previous proofers had missed.

She was also a minister's wife and she carried out that "position" beautifully. I doubt you could find any person who would say a negative thing about my mom in all the churches in which she and my dad served. She displayed grace, poise, and a servant's heart that impacted many throughout the years.

Mom also had a big impact on me, along with my older brother and sister. No matter what we did, whether she approved or not, her love for us never faltered. Her steadfast faith in her Savior was a clear example to us. Through her we knew what a walk with Him should look like. She taught us that if a job was worth doing, it was worth doing well. She often said, "Once a task has begun, never leave it 'til it's done. Whether it be great or small, do it well or not at all."

To see this amazing woman begin to falter mentally and emotionally was very difficult. It was a very slow process with her. I often said that I felt like I lost her one inch at a time over the years.

The day came when we had to move her into nursing care at the retirement center where my parents were living. We visited her weekly and never knew what to expect when we entered her room. There were times she was coherent and we could enjoy our time together. There were other days when her emotional and mental state made it very difficult to converse. She was often agitated and upset over something that had occurred that day and nothing we could say would make a difference. It was on those days that I left her room with a heavy heart, frustrated that I had been unable to calm her spirit.

But nothing prepared me for the day when I entered her room and it was obvious that she didn't have a clue as to who I was. The blank expression on her face, with no hint of recognition, was something I had never seen before. I remember sitting down beside her and trying to carry on a conversation, only to have her interrupt me and ask me what my name was and why I was there. I explained to her that I was her daughter, but her only answer was, "Oh."

I walked out of that facility with tears running down my face, and the realization that the mother I loved so dearly for so many years didn't know me. The mother who had stood beside me through thick and thin, who often told me how much she loved me and how proud she was of me, was now lost in a world that I couldn't understand and couldn't enter.

Visiting was more difficult after that experience. Not because I loved her any less, but because the pain of losing the Mom I knew was so great. I learned over time that I could still visit with her, but that our relationship had been changed. I was now an acquaintance instead of family. I celebrated on the days when she seemed to know who I was and fought tears on the days when she didn't.

Life isn't always wrapped up with a pretty bow, is it? Sometimes we are thrown into what seems like a deep abyss and there is darkness all around us. It's often at those times though, when God decides to bless us with one of His miracle moments. But as I shared yesterday, if we are too busy with our day-to-day activities to notice His hand at work in our lives, we just might miss it. Today might be the day so make sure you are paying attention!

My Jesus Prayer

Jesus, sometimes life's circumstances cause such deep pain that it can't even be explained. Please hold me, Jesus, during these times, but help me to be watching for those moments when You display Your power in a mighty way!

LUANN GERIG FULTON

DAY 7

Miracle Moments III

I will praise you, Lord, with all my heart; I will tell of all the marvelous things you have done (Psalm 9:1).

If I am completely honest, I had mixed feelings on Thursday, August 13th, 2009 when I received a phone call informing me that my mom had taken a turn for the worse. As I drove to be by her bedside, I really wasn't sure how to pray. The thought of losing my mother overwhelmed me, but the realization that in death she would have a new, whole body and mind with Jesus was healing to my soul. She had made it clear to us as we grew up that her focus was on her Lord and Savior and that she was willing to do whatever He asked of her. She had shared with me that in every decision she made, she wanted to make sure that it honored her Jesus and would have a positive impact on eternity. Knowing that was her desire, I knew that it was selfish of me to want her to remain on this earth. I knew of no one else more deserving to be welcomed into heaven with the words, "Well done, my good and faithful servant."

I entered her room and the scene was hard to observe. The nurses were telling us that she had suffered another stroke and could no longer swallow or speak. Her eyes stared blankly at the ceiling and there was no recognition on her part that her family was by her side. We did our best to keep our conversation on a positive note, not knowing for sure whether or not she could hear us.

Then, out of the blue and much to my surprise, I saw her eyes begin to move. Not only were they moving but they were actually following me as I walked around the room. I remember thinking that maybe I wasn't seeing clearly or that it was just my imagination, but when I looked again, it was clear that I was looking into the face of the Mom I had known for so many years. Even though she couldn't speak, it was obvious that she was trying to convey a message to me.

Through my tears I looked at her and said, "Mom, you know everything that's going on right now, don't you?" And, as unbelievable as it seemed at the moment, with everything she had left in her, she shook her head yes and attempted the slightest smile. I moved to the end of her bed, and once again, her eyes followed my every move.

I realized at that point that I more than likely had a very small window of opportunity to talk to her, so I knew exactly what I wanted to say. I looked into her beautiful eyes and said, "Mom, I just want you to know how much I love you." No sooner had the words left my mouth than my mom did something that I will never forget. She winked at me. I couldn't believe it! In that instant, I knew that God had performed this miracle moment so that my mom could tell me that she loved me one last time. She couldn't speak but she could wink, and what a gift that was to me.

Just as quickly as the miracle happened, it was over. Her eyes glazed back over and she was back in the world that I could not enter. But at that point, I knew that it wouldn't be long until she would meet her Jesus face-to-face.

Two days later, her family who had gone before her, along with her Lord and Savior Jesus Christ, greeted my mom on the streets of gold in heaven. No more anxiety. No more confusion. She was finally whole.

Miracle. It may be an overused word in our vocabulary, but for me, it is the only word that is appropriate for this experience. I have no doubt that it was an act of God. It was truly amazing, extraordinary, and unexpected.

What amazes me about this event is the fact that the Creator of the universe, the King of Kings, Lord of Lords, my Jesus, cared enough about me to bless me with this miracle. I didn't deserve it and I surely didn't do anything to earn it, but He gave me this blessing. He knows me so well and knew what occurrence would be miraculous to me. He orchestrated this miracle moment not only to remind me of my mom's love for me, but to whisper in my ear that I am also His child whom He dearly loves. He wanted me to know that He would hold me in His arms through the difficult days that followed.

Do you want to see miracles happen today? Look around you. Be watchful. I think that too often we are looking for an earth-shattering miracle to take place and we miss the miracle moments. You may not see a withered hand healed, but you just might experience a blessing far greater than you could ever imagine!

My Jesus Prayer

> *Jesus, thank You so much for shining Your light in my darkest moments. Help me to rest in Your care when sorrow overwhelms me, but keep me mindful that Your blessings may be right around the bend on my journey with You.*

DAY 8

A Look Within

So now I am giving you a new commandment: Love each other. Just as I have loved you, you should love each other. Your love for one another will prove to the world that you are my disciples (John 13:34-35).

My husband and I had an interesting conversation one day. I saw a picture of a man that we know and I commented as to how much I thought he had aged. Dan looked at the picture and said, "Well, he looks older because his hair is gray and thinning on top and he has a ruddy complexion." Then he paused for a few seconds and said, "Wait, I just described me!" We both had a good laugh over his realization. I have to admit that I had also thought his description fit him perfectly too, but after thirty-six years of marriage, I know there are times to keep my mouth shut!

Why is it that it is easy for us to see the flaws and imperfections in those around us, but difficult to see those things in us that don't measure up? As I'm sure you know, whenever we are leading up to an election, we are bombarded with political ads in which one candidate does their best to slaughter the reputation of their opponent. This is all done in hopes that the other person's shortcomings will look worse than theirs.

Unfortunately, it isn't just politicians that play this game; we often see the same thing in the Christian community. Instead of making sure we are spending time praying, reading God's Word, and listening to the Holy Spirit so that we know how *we* should be living, we spend our time attacking others, hoping that making them look worse will somehow make us look better. I think we somehow think that the louder we yell out the imperfections of others, the more spiritual we will appear to those around us. Regrettably, all this does is show that we are all just sinners saved by grace.

In Psalm 16:8 we read; *"I know the Lord is always with me. I will not be shaken, for he is right beside me."* As I contemplate these words, I realize that it is when my eyes are not on Him that I'm more tempted to lash out at others. Why? Because when my eyes are on me, and I realize how imperfect and weak I am, it is much easier to feel shaken and panicky. And as a result my need to feel better about myself drives me to want to make others look worse.

Will you join me today in striving to keep our eyes on the Lord instead? I happen to believe that if we make that a priority, we won't be so quick to attack those around us. We need to remember that others won't want to hear about our Jesus, if the words that come out of our mouth are hurtful. Just as it is always a relief to have the political ads come to an end, what a relief it might be to those around us if we got off the warpath too!

My Jesus Prayer

*Jesus, forgive me for those times when I have
degraded someone else to make myself look better.
Help me to remember that my words need to build
others up, instead of tearing them down.*

DAY 9
In the Meantime...

Give all your worries and cares to God, for he cares about you (1 Peter 5:7).

Pain. I have decided that I don't much like it. It isn't something I ask for, wish for, or enjoy. I have talked to people who say they have rarely, if ever, even taken an aspirin because they just don't experience pain, not even a headache. I can't imagine being that way: going through life without discomfort.

The word *pain* has come out of my mouth often due to a condition I have called Hypermobility Syndrome which is a form of Ehlers Danlos. The worst part of this syndrome is that there is nothing that can be done to cure it; only supportive care for the pain can be given.

If you have read much of my previous writings, you know that I try to be as transparent as possible with my readers. I believe God has called me to share my journey and the things that He needs to chip away in me to make me more like Him, so if I am going to be honest with you, I need to tell you that many of my days are a struggle. I have days when despair overwhelms me and self-pity rears its ugly head. I sometimes find it very difficult to slap a smile on my face so the world doesn't know what and how I am feeling.

What has amazed me is the fact that Jesus loves me through every second of every day. He doesn't desert me, or condemn me, or say that He is disappointed in me. Instead, He holds me and comforts me in the darkness. But I have begun to see that because He does love me so much, He doesn't want me to stay in this state of mind. He wants me to see my life's detours from a new perspective.

Jesus' first gentle reminder came to me in my devotional reading one day. In 2 Corinthians 6:3-10, I read these words from Paul, *"We live in such a way that no one will stumble because of us, and no one will find fault with our ministry. In everything we do, we show that we are true ministers of God. We patiently endure troubles and hardships and calamities of every kind. We have been beaten, been put in prison, faced angry mobs, worked to exhaustion, endured sleepless nights, and gone without food. We prove ourselves by our purity, our understanding, our patience, our kindness, by the Holy Spirit within us, and by our sincere love. We faithfully preach the truth. God's power is working in us. We use the weapons of righteousness in the right hand for attack and the left hand for defense. We serve God whether people honor us or despise us, whether they slander us or praise us. We are honest, but they call us impostors. We are ignored, even though we are well known. We live close to death, but we are still alive. We have been beaten, but we have not been killed. Our hearts ache, but we always have joy. We are poor, but we give spiritual riches to others. We own nothing, and yet we have everything."*

Even in the worst of conditions, Paul had joy. Nothing that happened to him could break his spirit or make him feel sorry for himself. He was willing to endure the worst of circumstances if it meant Christ's kingdom would be expanded. Paul didn't let anything stop him from spreading the good news to those who needed to hear it.

Jesus' second reminder to me came from a dear pastor friend of mine who also lives in pain. His story and mine have many similarities so we can often understand what the other is experiencing. In an e-mail to me, he wrote these words, "I guess the Lord believes we can both handle pain, surely more than we want. I think of His pain for me on the cross and I feel humbled to think I complain to Him about my pain. We must just rest in His care, for He asks us to cast all our cares upon Him."

His words touched me to the core. To think that my Jesus, because of His love for me and every other person, willingly hung on a cross and endured pain way beyond anything I can imagine doesn't make sense to me. I would be willing to endure pain for someone I love, but to do it for those who hate me seems unfathomable. He died for those who spit on Him, beat Him, and crucified Him. And to bring it closer to home, He died for those, like me, who take their eyes off Him, causing self-pity and despair to overwhelm them.

I can't say that I'm not still struggling in this area of my life, because the pain continues and I'm definitely a work in progress. But if what I'm going through can help just one person to refocus on Jesus and realize just how much He loves them, I think it will all be worth it. I so desperately look forward to the day when, like Paul, I can say, *"I live in such a way that no one will stumble because of me, and no one will find fault with my ministry. In everything I do, I show that I am a true minister of God."* I have a long way to go to get there, but in the meantime, I'm going to cast my cares upon Him and trust Him for the strength and peace to live for Him today. He promises to give me His power every day, every hour, every minute as He continues to mold me and make me look more like Him.

I don't know what you are going through today. You may also be struggling and feel like you are all alone. You may be experiencing physical, mental, or emotional pain. You may have the pain of a broken marriage, loss of a loved one, or maybe the loss of a treasured friendship. Don't forget that you are not alone! Jesus promises to walk your journey with you and give you what is needed for today. Believe me, whatever you are going through, He has been there and understands every emotion you are feeling. Let Him hold you today and remind you just how much He loves you. Victory may be just around the corner; but in the meantime, cast all of your burdens on Him. Remember, Jesus promises to give you His power every day, every hour, every minute as He continues to mold you and make you look more like Him.

My **Jesus Prayer**

> *Jesus, thank You for being with me every moment of every day. Help me to cast all of my pain and hurt on You and rely on Your strength, not my own, as I strive to become more like You.*

DAY 10

Get Up!

Work willingly at whatever you do, as though you were working for the Lord rather than for people (Colossians 3:23).

We live in the country. Some would say we live *way* out in the country. We've even had friends tell us that we live in the "boonies"—wherever that is. Whatever others may choose to call it, we call it God's country. We love having farmland surrounding us. Every other year we have corn encompassing our home and I just love the feeling of having this "fence" around our property. It's just pure heaven.

Even though I love where we live, I wouldn't want to be a farmer. I can't imagine what they go through, year after year, being so dependent on the weather. Will we get too much rain or not enough? Will it be too cool or too hot? Will some insect wreak havoc with the crops and destroy what has been grown or will a windstorm blow through and flatten what was once standing tall?

That is just more stress than I want to experience, but the farmers in our area seem to take it all in stride. It's just part of their job as they figure out what should be planted and when it should be planted. They do everything in their power to have an abundant crop. One thing I have noticed is that they realize they can't wait to plant their seeds until the perfect day comes along. More than likely, no day will be perfect. There will always be something that isn't exactly as it should be. Since a perfect day may never come, they have to move forward and begin planting because they realize that none of the seeds will grow unless they are in the ground.

I came across an interesting verse in the Bible one day. It is Ecclesiastes 11:4: *"Farmers who wait for perfect weather never plant. If they watch every cloud, they never harvest."* How true this is! If they want to harvest their crop, they know they have to first get it in the dirt!

Fortunately because I'm not a farmer, I guess this verse doesn't pertain to me, right? Wrong! I think we all can learn a lesson from these words. How many times in our lives do we not attempt something because we are just waiting for the perfect time to do it? Instead of moving forward we stand still because we just don't think everything is in place to accomplish what we know Jesus is telling us to do. Our waiting for just the right time often means inactivity in our spiritual life.

If we wait for just that perfect time to read our Bible, we will probably never begin. If we wait for that perfect church to come along, where there are no problems and no hypocrites, we will never find one. If we wait for that perfect ministry to get involved in, we will never serve. If we wait until our home is in perfect order, we will probably never invite anyone in for fellowship.

What happens when we wait? We miss out on showers of blessings that Jesus wants to give us. We miss out on times of wonderful fellowship as we come alongside our brothers and sisters in Christ. We miss out on the times of harvest, when our hard work pays off and we see results that will make a difference in eternity.

What are you waiting for? Is the Lord asking you to do something, but you are sitting on your haunches, just waiting for the perfect time? I want to encourage you today to get up and start moving. Get up and dust off your Bible and start reading, even if you only have a few minutes. Get up on Sunday morning and begin checking out area churches. Don't look for perfection; look for God's love and power to be alive and well. Get up and begin seeing where you can volunteer to make a difference in the lives of others. Get up and pick up your phone and invite others into your home to show them that you care so they will want to hear about your Jesus.

Just get up and start planting seeds, even if the conditions aren't perfect. You may be amazed at the bountiful harvest you will be blessed with when you just get up.

My **Jesus Prayer**

> *Jesus, it is so easy for me to want to sit on the sidelines, hoping that everything will just fall into place on its own. Help me to not be satisfied with doing nothing, but willing to get up and begin doing something!*

DAY 11

Feeling Loved

When God's people are in need, be ready to help them. Always be eager to practice hospitality (Romans 12:13).

It was the eve of New Year's Eve and I received the following text: "Have no plans for New Year's Eve so checking in to see if some of our friends are in the same boat and would like to come to our home and bring in the New Year, or close to it. Around 6:30-ish. Bring a finger food. We'll supply drinks, bean and salsa dip with chips. Just text and let us know if it works or doesn't." What an awesome message to receive! We had planned to spend a quiet night at home to bring in the New Year, but who can turn down such a wonderful invitation as this?

My mind immediately began turning as to what I could fix to take to share with these friends. There was an instant excitement in the air. We felt so honored to be asked to this home. The evening went from being mundane to eventful. What made the difference? Someone made the decision to show hospitality.

Hospitality. I could be wrong, but I'm afraid it's a word and practice that isn't used much anymore. We are all so wrapped up in our own schedules that we use any available excuse as to why we shouldn't display hospitality. Our home isn't big enough or nice enough. Our schedule is too busy to invite friends or we think our lives are so boring that no one would want to come. Our kids don't behave well enough, or we don't want other misbehaving children in our home. We aren't good enough cooks and we sure don't know how to put together a fancy meal that would impress others. I could go on and on.

The home we were invited to was not a mansion. In fact, our friends had purchased this home and were in the process of remodeling it. There wasn't even a kitchen counter yet. When the hostess needed water, she had to go to the bathroom to get it from a faucet there. Card tables were set up for the food and for places for some to sit. We didn't have a twelve-course meal with fine china and goblets.

What we *did* have was an extremely warm welcome as we entered their front door. Their smiles conveyed to us the words, *we sure are glad you could come*. We were given a tour of their home and shown what they had already done and were told of their future plans. We were invited to sit down with them and enjoy wonderful finger foods that all had brought to share.

One of the best things about the evening was that we had the privilege of meeting three couples who we hadn't known before. Within just a short time, all twelve of us were talking, laughing and playing games together that brought the "kid" out in all of us.

This precious couple could have used numerous excuses as to why they couldn't invite us, but instead they chose to display Christ to each one of us. I don't believe there is anyone on this earth that doesn't need to know that someone else loves them and cares about them and there is no greater way to accomplish this than through hospitality.

Who could you invite to your home to show Christ's love? I'm sure the list is endless. If the thought scares you to death, ask a couple others to do it with you and the four of you can host an evening together. Start with just a few people until your confidence is built up. Just remember to keep it simple and easy. People could care less how fancy things are; they just want to be loved.

We came away from our New Year's Eve celebration that year feeling very blessed. Blessed not because of material things, but because of something far more valuable. Thanks, Phil and Kat, for giving us an evening worth much more than anything money could buy—an evening of being loved.

My Jesus Prayer

Jesus, thank You for friends who know what it means to bless others by showing hospitality. Help me to learn from them and begin to touch the lives of others by showing them love. Help me to remember that they won't want to hear about my Jesus if they don't feel my love first.

DAY 12

Is The Sky Falling?

The Lord gives his people strength. The Lord blesses them with peace (Psalm 29:11).

We sure live in a mixed up world, don't we? All we have to do is watch the evening news to make our stomach turn. Murders, suicides, school and airport shootings, wars, and ISIS threats are just a few of the headlines that can easily upset us.

If the evening news doesn't depress us enough, just log onto any social media and read everyone's opinions on these world happenings. I'll be honest, there are times when I want to post these words under someone's rant, "The sky is falling, the sky is falling!" So far I've held myself back.

Am I troubled by all of these events? You bet I am. We are living in a very dark world in which Satan is attacking at every level. It is a time when we have to be alert and on guard so we don't succumb to his attacks. I believe these events should escalate our endeavors to reach as many people as we can for Jesus before it is too late. We, as Christians, need to rise up and make sure we aren't just talking the talk, but walking the walk each and every day so that others see Him in us.

But (and you knew a "but" was coming) I am really troubled by the "sky is falling" attitude of many believers. While we should be concerned and doing all we can to make our world better, we should still have the peace from our Jesus living within us. We should still know in whom we have our faith and trust, and rest in that assurance. If we don't, why in the world would unbelievers want what we have?

I've talked to Christians who are almost paralyzed in fear. They don't want to go anywhere because they might be harmed or exposed to Ebola. The news on their TV is playing continually, as their minds are deluged with one negative story after another.

Our church had a good old-fashioned hymn sing one evening and I thoroughly enjoyed it. Don't get me wrong, I love the newer music too, but I also love the hymns and the beautiful harmonies that rise up to the rafters. One of the very familiar hymns really stopped me in my tracks as we sang, and I struggled to think about much else the rest of the evening. There all of us were, singing that it was well with our souls. We were singing that no matter what happened in our lives, it would be well with our souls.

As we sang, all I could think of was, *is it really well with my soul?* With all the turmoil going on around me, can I honestly say that it is well with my soul? Even though Satan is throwing darts left and right at me and at the rest of the world, do I still trust Christ enough to have a soul that is well?

If not, I sure don't have much to offer unbelievers. If I'm just as frazzled as they are, if I'm continually acting as if there is no hope, I sure better not try to tell them about my Jesus. If I do try to talk to them, it won't take long for them to call me a hypocrite, a label I would deserve.

Time is running out and the day is going to come when instead of the sky falling, it will open up and Jesus will make His return. Many, many people need to hear about His return and what He has prepared in heaven for those who have accepted Him as their Lord and Savior. It's up to us to let them know, so let's make sure as we walk, talk, and share that our soul is well so they can see His peace in us.

My Jesus Prayer

Jesus, it is so easy for me to become overwhelmed with fear as the world seems out of control. Help me to put my trust in You, allowing You to fill me with Your peace which surpasses all understanding.

DAY 13
An Act Of Kindness

We prove ourselves by our purity, our understanding, our patience, our kindness, by the Holy Spirit within us, and by our sincere love (2 Corinthians 6:6).

If a person has to spend hours in a hospital, having a good place to eat ends up being the bright spot in their day. I've been to hospitals where eating the food just might make you a patient there, but I have discovered that isn't the case at one of the hospitals in our area. I have been pleasantly surprised at the variety and quality of food that is available in their dining room. There are many items to choose from at a very affordable price and I have never had a bad meal (and I have lost count of the number of meals I have consumed there).

One of the times when a family member was a patient in this hospital, there was one area of the cafeteria from which I selected most of my food and a gentleman working there was very personable. He always greeted me with a smile and asked what he could prepare for me. After I had been there for almost a week, I told him what a great job the staff was doing. I also told him how much easier their service was making my time there. Just knowing I had a nice place to eat and relax helped. He seemed to genuinely appreciate the compliment and commenced to prepare my food.

About a week later we once again made our way to the dining room to eat. I was beyond tired on this particular evening. The last twenty-four hours had been a roller coaster ride of constantly changing reports from multiple doctors and it had taken its toll. I was worn out mentally, emotionally, and physically.

I approached the counter that was now very familiar to me. The man greeted me with his usual smile and asked what I wanted to eat. I told him and he stepped back to prepare it. As he was cooking, he looked at me and said, "You look exhausted." I usually try to cover my tiredness in public, but obviously wasn't hiding it very well at that time. I shook my head and said that yes, I was very tired and felt a tear escape my eye.

He continued to cook and I noticed that at one point he went into a back room for a moment, but then returned to finish up my meal. A few seconds later, I realized that a woman had come up and was standing next to me. I didn't know her and just figured she was also waiting on an order. But when the gentleman handed me my food, this woman looked at me and said, "Your food is free tonight." I looked up at the man behind the counter and he just shook his head yes and said it was on him. He just wanted to do something to encourage me.

At that moment, all I could do was cry. Believe me when I say that the floodgates were opened. I had not allowed myself to cry or become emotional at all during the days we had been in the hospital. I knew I had to remain strong for my family members and there just wasn't time to "feel" anything, but this man's simple act of kindness had broken through my thick exterior and touched me to the core. I shook my head as I wept and whispered, "Thank you."

This man, and I didn't even know his name, took time out of his busy day to lift my spirits. He purposely chose to act kindly in a way that helped lighten the heaviness I felt. He could have easily been so wrapped up in his own life that he wouldn't have noticed my demeanor, but he took the time to touch the soul of another.

This incident was a wonderful reminder to me that I need to be more sensitive to those with whom I come in contact. I need to be more intentional in performing acts of kindness throughout my day to encourage those who are disheartened. So many people just need to know that someone cares, that they are noticed, and that there is hope.

Who can you encourage today? What can you do to lift someone's spirit? Be alert and be aware and be the one who lightens the load of others. That's what Jesus wants us to do, and I believe that each time we listen to His prompting, He will allow us to not only bless, but to be blessed in return. Remember, others won't want to hear about your Jesus, unless they see Jesus in you first. They are watching. What will they see in you today?

My Jesus Prayer

> *Jesus, help me today to take my eyes off myself and use them to see the faces of those around me. They may need to know that someone cares. Let that someone be me.*

LUANN GERIG FULTON

DAY 14

In the Eyes of My Beholders

The Lord is my strength and shield. I trust him with all my heart. He helps me, and my heart is filled with joy. I burst out in songs of thanksgiving (Psalm 28:7).

Confession time. I'm not a very trusting person. I tend to be a skeptic, someone who makes a person prove to me that they can be trusted before I believe in them. I think that sometimes it is a good way to be, and sometimes it's not. I'm not completely sure why I'm that way, except for the fact that I don't like to be hurt. Trusting someone opens up the possibility that they may let me down, and as a result cause me pain.

Because of this, it's probably no surprise that I struggle at times with trusting my Jesus too. Even though I know beyond a shadow of a doubt that His ways and timing are perfect, I still fail to trust. But I think my reasoning for not always trusting Him is different than it is with humans. It's not that I don't trust Him because I'm afraid I'll get hurt; I don't trust Him because I'm afraid I might not get my way. Realizing this makes me squirm a little bit.

I've heard it said that "a relationship without trust is like a car without gas: You can stay in it all you want, but it won't go anywhere." I could own a sports car and buff it until it shone. When my friends saw it they would admire my beautiful car. But if I turned the key and it wasn't filled with fuel to make it run, it would lose a lot of its luster in the eyes of the beholder.

The same is true for me. I can say I'm a Christian, dress in the finest clothes, and even darken the door of a church three times a week, but if my life isn't centered on trusting the One who fuels me, I will also lose luster in the eyes of my beholders. Those with whom I come in contact will soon realize that I am just an empty shell without anything in which they would have interest. Why would they want what I have if my relationship with Jesus remains stagnant and doesn't grow or deepen?

I think it comes down to this very basic fact: To grow in Christ, you and I *must* trust. It isn't an option. It isn't something we can plan to do in the future when we think we will be older and wiser. The time is now. Let's allow Him to be our fuel as we willingly obey His leading. It may be a little scary and even a little tiring, but I'm confident that with Him we will never run out of gas!

My Jesus Prayer

Jesus, help me have the courage to put my complete trust in You. I know others are watching, and if I want to tell them about my Jesus, they need to see me in total obedience to You. Help me to grow my roots deeper in You today.

LUANN GERIG FULTON

DAY 15
A Work in Progress

Trust in the Lord with all your heart; do not depend on your own understanding. Seek his will in all you do, and he will show you which path to take (Proverbs 3:5-6).

I shared with you yesterday about the topic of trust. Sometimes it's easier to write about something than it is to live it.

On a Tuesday morning, May 6th, 2014, my father-in-law, Carl, lost his seven-week battle with acute leukemia, but gained the opportunity to walk on streets of gold. We had prayed for healing and our prayers were answered, but not with the earthly healing for which we had hoped.

Thirty-six hours later, our precious grandson was born. What a blessing to hold him in my arms for the first time and fall head over heels in love with him. He has been wonderfully created by my God, a perfect masterpiece. What an incredible miracle! What a priceless gift.

To be honest, during that thirty-six-hour period between losing Carl and welcoming our grandson, I was angry. To me, the timing of all of this stunk. None of it made any sense. Why in the world would God take my father-in-law on the same day that my daughter was to enter the hospital 160 miles away? I felt pulled in too many directions. I wanted to be home to be with my mother-in-law and help with all of the funeral preparations, but I also wanted to be with my daughter and son-in-law and be present for our first grandchild's birth.

We made the decision to stay in town that afternoon to meet with the funeral director and make the necessary plans for the service. Due to the fact that we owned a catering service, which employed two of my brothers-in-law, our schedule required that the funeral would have to be held off until the following week. With details in place, we took off that evening to make the trip to the hospital where our daughter had been admitted.

Her labor lasted over twenty-five hours and was very difficult. I paced the halls of the hospital pleading with God to make sure she had a safe delivery with a healthy baby. To be honest, if I had ranked my level of trust as I paced those halls, I wouldn't have received a very high score. Panic was overtaking me and all sorts of scenarios filled my mind. My husband and I felt like we were on an emotional roller coaster and we were both exhausted. Again, I questioned God. The timing of these events just didn't make sense.

Even with my lack of trust, God answered my pleas and blessed us with a healthy baby and daughter. The relief that swept through me when I received a picture of our beautiful grandson by text from my son-in-law in the operating room was indescribable.

But when I had him placed in my arms about an hour later, God's timing made perfect sense. At that moment, I understood that this baby had been given to us as a sign from God of His faithfulness. He gave us hope at a time when hurt filled us. He gave refreshment to our parched and weary souls.

Little did I know at that moment that God had one more sign of His perfect timing to show us. We had not been told our grandson's name before his birth. So as we stood in our daughter's hospital room and as my husband held this precious one, our daughter, through tears, told us that his name was Elias Carl Yang, named after my father-in-law. They had selected his name even before Carl's illness, having no clue what would happen in the meantime.

They didn't know, but God did. To us, all of this made no sense, but to Him it made perfect sense. It's at moments such as this that I get frustrated with myself because I rely on my own understanding instead of His, and my own strength instead of His unending power.

I'm so thankful that I serve a God who loves me, even with my lack of faith and trust. I want to rely fully on Him, not wavering when the winds begin to blow, so I continue onward, taking each day as it comes and striving to look more like Him in everything that I do. I'm definitely a work in progress with a lot of "remodeling" to do to make sure others see Him in me. That's my goal, and I hope it is yours too!

My Jesus Prayer

> *Jesus, I so desperately want to stand firm in You when strong winds begin to blow. Help me to remain strong, trusting You to mold me into the person that You created me to be.*

DAY 16
Chill Pill

Those who are dominated by the sinful nature think about sinful things, but those who are controlled by the Holy Spirit think about things that please the Spirit (Romans 8:5).

It was a Sunday evening and my husband and I had just returned from church. We have a tradition that includes eating popcorn every Sunday night, so we changed our clothes and went into our family room to devour our delectable delight. Before I could even take one bite, we both heard a very loud boom. I looked at Dan and said, "It sounded like a car just hit our house." We both immediately jumped up and went through our home, room by room looking for the reason for this unexpected interruption. Once we entered our bedroom, our question was answered. Yes indeed, we now had a "redecorated" wall in our room.

Dan took off for the front door and yelled for me to call 911. Fortunately, by the time he was outside, the occupants of the car had managed to get out and were heading toward him. While I filled the dispatcher in on the phone, a young man, woman, and a seven-year-old girl entered our living room. They were naturally very shaken, but very thankfully, not injured. Within minutes our driveway looked like a carnival, with flashing lights penetrating the darkness as many local responders invaded our home.

I have heard many stories of this type of event happening to homes that are close to a road, but we live in the country and our home sits quite a ways off the road. Of all the natural disasters that I had imagined could at some point damage our property, a car running into our home wasn't even on the list. But it had now happened, and we had bricks lying all over our bedroom to prove it.

Monday morning came and any previous plans we had for the day (and for much of our week) were now changed. The hole in our wall needed to be secured to insure that the weather and unwanted varmints stayed outside where they belonged. Hours were spent cleaning up debris and securing the wall studs to be somewhat back in place to support the wall. Insurance agents were talked to and a contractor was called for an estimate.

Throughout that week though, God just kept reminding me of His faithfulness. There were so many what-if's to this event. The driver skimmed an electrical pole as she left the road. If she had hit the pole head on, there would have most definitely been injuries. There were trees on our property that, if hit, wouldn't have blessed the occupants with a good result. The car hit the end of our home, just inches from the corner of our all brick exterior, which I believe also saved them from a far different outcome. And just minutes before the car made impact with our brick, I had been standing on the other side of the wall where the car entered.

Coincidences? I don't think so. God was definitely watching out for everyone involved in this somewhat-scary incident. For some reason, God chose to protect all of us and allow us to come through the event relatively unscathed. I know that others have had unexpected events occur and the outcome was not so nice, so I feel very blessed that what was hurt in this situation was not eternal.

A home can be repaired and furnishings can be replaced. The "stuff" that we have isn't going to heaven or hell, so getting upset and allowing it to ruin our attitude, our day, or week is really a waste of our energy. It is easy to let things that have no eternal consequence affect our moods. The result is that our testimony to those around us becomes less than what it should be. It's sad that we often get more upset over the loss of a material object than we do about the loss of a soul to hell.

I think it comes down to our focus. Is it on making sure that those we meet know Jesus as their Lord and Savior, or is it on what we need to do to hold onto our earthly treasures? The one focus will have a part in helping others spend eternity in heaven with our Lord and Savior.

The other just may hinder others from hearing the good news, causing them to spend eternity in hell.

What will you choose to be upset about today? As situations arise, why not ask yourself this question: *Is this going to heaven or hell*? If it's not, then why not take a "chill pill" and give thanks to the Lord for sparing you from an event that has an eternal consequence. Allow Him to lower your stress level by focusing on what is eternal. We need to remember that it is usually much easier if we hold things loosely in our hands than if He has to pry them from our fists.

My Jesus Prayer

*Jesus, help me to realize that the material things
I possess are not important. Help my attitude not
be swayed by the things around me, but instead be
constantly focused on only things that have an eternal
consequence.*

LUANN GERIG FULTON

DAY 17
A Beach Experience I

And you yourself must be an example to them by doing good works of every kind. Let everything you do reflect the integrity and seriousness of your teaching (Titus 2:7).

Living in Indiana affords us the opportunity to experience something that not everyone in the country gets to experience, and that is four seasons. Each year we usually witness the changes around us as we go through spring, summer, fall, and winter. I like spring because it means summer isn't far behind, and that is my favorite season of all. Fall usually isn't too bad, but it means winter isn't far off, which is my least favorite time of year. I have to work really hard at not constantly complaining during the cold winter days, but you will rarely hear me complain about the heat. I'm truly a summer person through and through.

It's probably not a surprise then that I love the beach. I love the sun, the sand, the breeze, and the sound of the waves crashing on the shore. I love it all! I was introduced to it when my family moved to California as I was growing up and I had the privilege of living in the Golden State for five-and-a-half years.

Once I had my driver's license, there was only one place I wanted to be on Saturdays. I would pick up my girlfriend, Susan, hop on the Santa Monica freeway and head for the water. No matter what had transpired during the week, those things were now ancient history; there was something so healing and renewing when we spent a day soaking up the rays.

The only glitch to the day was that we usually went on Saturdays and that was always cleaning day at my house. There was no way around it. If the house wasn't cleaned, I wouldn't see a glimpse of heaven that day. My mom was a pretty easygoing person, but I knew the rules, and that meant things had to be done before I was allowed to leave.

Sometimes it stinks to have to be responsible, doesn't it? Sometimes we just want to have the fun in life without all the work involved. Because of our selfish nature, it's easy to allow ourselves to navigate toward what makes us happy and what makes us feel good at the moment. We often feel that if we just ignore those things for which we are responsible, they will fade away or someone else will do them for us. But unfortunately, at some point someone will suffer for our laziness, whether it is us or someone else, because eventually our actions will take their toll.

Over the next few days I'm going to be sharing more in depth of my beach experiences and how they relate to our everyday life. There are several analogies that I think the Lord can use to help us focus on what our walk with Christ should resemble.

Today I want to urge you to take a look at each of your responsibilities and whether or not you are fulfilling those with a servant's heart. Is your family suffering because you would rather just do what makes you happy instead of making sure their needs are met? Is your boss happy to see you walk into work each day because he or she knows you will do your very best for the company during the hours you are there? Or do the other employees have to do extra work to cover for your lack of motivation?

As Christians, we need to always keep in mind that when we work we really aren't working for man, we are working for our Jesus. If we take our responsibilities seriously and do what God has set before us, our time at the "beach" will be even more heavenly!

My **Jesus Prayer**

> *Jesus, You have set before me the tasks that need to be accomplished today. Help me to do them as if You were my "boss" for the day. Maybe that will help me remember that everything that I do, should be done for Your honor and glory!*

LUANN GERIG FULTON

DAY 18
A Beach Experience II

But when you pray, go away by yourself, shut the door behind you, and pray to your Father in private. Then your Father, who sees everything, will reward you (Matthew 6:6).

As I shared yesterday, once my house cleaning chores were done on those Saturday mornings in California, my goal was to get to the beach as soon as possible. Traffic usually wasn't an issue in getting there because Saturday mornings weren't normally a high traffic time. Within thirty minutes we were usually pulling into the parking lot, ready for a taste of heaven.

The first decision was always where we were going to lay our towels. We would look for a spot that wasn't already crowded and close enough to the water to hear the waves. But depending on what time of day it was and how hot the sun was, getting to that perfect spot might be a little painful.

If you've never been to the beach, you may not know that the sand can become very hot. If we decided to take off our flip-flops to trek across the sand, it wasn't uncommon to see us walk for a while and then stop. Unfortunately, just stopping didn't lessen the pain on the bottoms of our feet. We would have to quickly bury our feet under the sand to find the coolness we required. We'd stand there long enough to cool off the soles of our feet, and then return to the hot sand. It took time to get where we wanted to be, but it was necessary to stop periodically to make sure we arrived at our destination.

This often happens in our daily walk too, doesn't it? It may not be hot sand that is causing us pain, but our daily experiences and responsibilities can easily cause us discomfort. At that point we usually have a choice. We can just keep pushing through, forcing ourselves to move forward, and allow the pain to intensify, or we can stop and take a few moments to bury ourselves under the protection of our Father and allow Him to bring coolness to our soul.

Beginning each day with the Lord before things heat up helps me handle my pain throughout the day. How soothing it is to know that when tough moments cause me to overheat in my daily walk, He is right there to cover me with His "sand" of comfort and coolness. All I have to do is take the time to stop, which isn't always easy for a person with a type A personality like me. When I do, it makes the remainder of my trek much more manageable and enjoyable.

If you feel the heat of the sand today, make it a point to stop even for just a few minutes. Ask your heavenly Father to cover you and soothe your tired, pain-filled soul. You just might be surprised how much easier your next steps will be after you have spent some time with Him.

My Jesus Prayer

> *Jesus, I know that today will more than likely have some hot spots, when I will feel the heat of the world on my shoulders. Help me to remember to take time to stop to allow You to bring coolness to my spirit and refreshment to my soul.*

DAY 19
A Beach Experience III

But keep alert at all times. And pray that you might be strong enough to escape these coming horrors and stand before the Son of Man (Luke 21:36).

The ocean. I'm just not sure I know the words to describe it. Its beauty is beyond words and the soothing effect that it can have on your soul is incredible. One can arrive feeling harried and stressed, but within minutes of feeling its spray and hearing its waves crashing onto the shore, can find peace and serenity.

However, it is important for those who enjoy its beauty to also understand its power. Like so many things in life, what can bring great joy can also bring danger and despair. The peril that occurs below the surface cannot be detected until the water encompasses a person, and if the swimmer is not prepared for the undertow, he or she can quickly lose their footing.

I call it the "washing machine" effect. This happened to me as a teenager when a wave crashed over me and at the same time the undertow was working to pull me away from the shore and farther out in the ocean. The result was that I felt like I was in a washing machine, being flipped and turned around until it was difficult to even stand back up. Water was pulling and pushing me from every direction and I can remember a few times when I wondered if I would ever break the surface of the water again. The key was to understand the power of the pull ahead of time and not fear it, but be prepared by knowing what it would take to regain my footing again.

There have been other times in my life when I was hundreds of miles away from any beach, but my life still felt like it was in a washing machine. Problems and stress were pulling and pushing me from every direction, and I can remember times when I wasn't sure I would ever see the surface of life again. I felt caught; encompassed by the turmoil around me, struggling to enjoy the beauty that was there because of the chaos and turbulence that overshadowed it.

I have come to realize that Satan wants to keep us in the "washing machine" for as long as he can. As long as we are in the middle of the mayhem, we will probably not be productive for the Lord. As long as he can keep us feeling overwhelmed, no peace will fill our souls. And as long as he can keep us feeling that there isn't any hope, he can keep us from trusting the One who *is* our hope.

Are you in the "washing machine" of life right now? The key to breaking the surface is to understand the power of the pull of Satan and not fear it, but be prepared by knowing God's Word to help you regain your footing. Our God is stronger than any rough current that Satan can send your way, but if you wait until you are in the midst of this tumultuous cycle, you may be pulled farther under. If you are in an upheaval now, rely on His power to help you regain your footing.

If you aren't experiencing chaos at the moment, use this time to fill your mind with God's Word to empower and strengthen you for Satan's next deceitful undertow. Remember, it isn't a matter of *if* Satan will attack, it is a matter of *when* Satan will attack. You must be prepared now, even if the water is currently calm.

My **Jesus Prayer**

Jesus, help me to be alert and watching today for Satan's attempts to put me into the "washing machine" of life. I know that You are much more powerful than he is, so help me to turn to You for strength so that I can keep my feet firmly planted in You.

LUANN GERIG FULTON

DAY 20
A Beach Experience IV

Get rid of all bitterness, rage, anger, harsh words, and slander, as well as all types of evil behavior. Instead, be kind to each other, tenderhearted, forgiving one another, just as God through Christ has forgiven you (Ephesians 4:31-32).

I shared yesterday about the "washing machine" experiences that occurred when I was in the ocean during my teen years and that continue to occur in my daily life. As I reflect on that further, it occurs to me that unfortunately, some experiences that happen in my life are a result of choices I have made. I have made decisions that I knew were not in line with the Lord's desire for my life, and as a result I have had to endure "washing machine" consequences. I have no one to blame but myself, and even though I have eventually repented and asked for forgiveness, I sometimes still have had to go through difficult days because of my choices in the past.

But what about those times when life suddenly throws dirt on us and we haven't done anything to deserve it? I remember many times when this literally happened to us as we soaked up the sun. Usually by midafternoon, other sun worshippers were beginning to pack things up and head for home. That was always fine with us because it just gave us more beach to enjoy. The problem arose when, especially on windy days, other beach goers shook out their towels to rid them of the sand and we would suddenly find ourselves covered with their unwanted grit. Instead of doing this away from those around them, they didn't seem to care if their actions affected us or not.

Just like we didn't deserve to be inundated with sand, there are times in all of our lives when we are suddenly thrown into a tailspin because of the actions of others. Family members, coworkers, acquaintances, and even people we don't know sometimes make wrong decisions that not only affect them, but us too. The "washing machine" experience isn't a result of our actions, but theirs. It feels natural to become angry, hurt, and ready to seek revenge.

Honesty moment. I struggle with this and sometimes cringe when I see the word *all* in our scripture for today. It would be so much easier if the word *some* was used instead, because my nature wants to hold onto at least some of my ill feelings towards those who have hurt me. I feel like they don't deserve my total forgiveness because what they did caused me pain; therefore they should now feel pain. But Christ is telling us that there is no room in our lives for feelings of revenge. We are commanded to forgive because He has forgiven us.

Is life spinning all around you today as a result of the sinful actions of others? Join me in trying to remember how much we have been forgiven, all of our faults and failures, and then let's forgive those who have caused us pain. I know it won't be easy, but if Christ endured the cross for our sins, I guess we can endure some "grit" for Him.

My Jesus Prayer

> *Jesus, forgive me for the times I have struggled to forgive those who have hurt me. Help me to be kind, tenderhearted, and loving to those with whom I come in contact. May I be always mindful that I do not answer for their actions, but I will answer for mine.*

LUANN GERIG FULTON

DAY 21
A Beach Experience V

And now, dear brothers and sisters, one final thing. Fix your thoughts on what is true, and honorable, and right, and pure, and lovely, and admirable. Think about things that are excellent and worthy of praise (Philippians 4:8).

I have been sharing for the past few days about my love for the beach and my memories of spending many days there during my teenage years. Those days have left me with priceless memories that I will cherish for the rest of my life. But each of those days, just like so many other wonderful moments, had to come to an end. Each time we went, we knew that our time was limited and that we would need to eventually head home and enter back into reality.

We also knew that each time we went, we had a choice to make as to when we would leave. As I stated earlier, traffic was never an issue going to the beach, especially if it was on a Saturday morning. Unfortunately, that usually wasn't the case by the afternoon. If we thought sensibly and left by midafternoon, traffic was usually fairly light and we returned home in good time. But if we procrastinated because we wanted to get just a few more rays, we inevitably ended up in bumper-to-bumper traffic. A trip that usually took around thirty minutes could often be drawn out for hours instead.

It's not like ending up in very slow moving traffic caught us off guard. We were smart enough to know there would be consequences to our choices. But even though we knew we would pay the price for staying longer at the beach, there were times we still chose to go against our better judgment and lag behind.

While this wasn't a sin, it sure reminds me of how many times in my life I made choices that I knew would have consequences; consequences that were sure to make life much more uncomfortable. There's a host of things like this: eating more than I should at a meal, which I know will drag my energy level down. Staying up later than I should, knowing that the lack of sleep will affect the next day. Or trying to cram just one more thing into my day, knowing full well it will eventually make me crankier and a not-so-nice person to be around.

Then there are those times when I know my decisions *are* sins, but yet I choose to make them anyway, knowing full well there will be consequences. Choosing to gossip and talk maliciously about someone, feeling justified at the moment but knowing that tearing someone down is never right in God's eyes. Choosing to watch a movie or TV show, or read a trashy novel that fills my mind with ungodly thoughts and only serves to tear down my mind and soul, which in turn takes my focus off Christ. Choosing to eat unhealthy foods on a consistent basis, knowing that my body is a temple and vessel for Him, and this only serves to worsen my health so I am not able to fully serve Him.

The problem is that I can usually justify those things as not being sins. I have no desire to rob a bank, shoot someone, steal from my neighbor, or even take the Lord's name in vain; and as long as I refrain from any of those *big* sins I must be okay, right? Unfortunately, I'm not sure that is how the Lord views my actions, and I'm confident my daily choices often cause Him pain. To be a fully devoted follower of Christ, He wants every part of us. Every decision and choice should be in line with His Word. When I fully realize that, I fall grossly short.

An innocent day at the beach can help us learn so many lessons and can give us an opportunity to evaluate where we are in our walk with Christ. Are we fulfilling our daily responsibilities with a servant's heart, or are we making others pick up the slack? Are we spending time each day with our heavenly Father to make sure we are prepared for whatever comes our way? Are we staying alert to Satan's attempts to grab hold of us and drag us under? Are we willing to forgive those who have caused us pain by their actions? Finally, are the choices and decisions we make each day fully in line with His Word?

I sure hope so. The time is coming when we will each see our Jesus face-to-face. That may be today, tomorrow, or weeks or years to come. For now, we need to make sure we are prepared for that time which will make a day at the beach pale in comparison. Let's do what He is asking of us now, so we will hear Him say, *"Well done, my good and faithful servant"* on that day!

My Jesus Prayer

Jesus, I so desperately want to make the right choices today; choices that will be in line with Your Word. May I serve You today to the best of my ability so that Your name will be glorified here on earth as I prepare to meet You face-to-face!

DAY 22
Staying Connected

As the deer longs for streams of water, so I long for you, O God. I thirst for God, the living God (Psalm 42:1-2a).

In 1971, my family moved to Van Nuys, California, which is wear I fell in love with the beach. I was getting ready to enter sixth grade and I did not handle the transition well. It is a difficult age for most children, and being taken from a very small, Midwestern town to a suburb of Los Angeles was overwhelming. I remember my first day of school as if it were yesterday. I walked into the school office, knowing no one, and asked where I was supposed to go. The secretary gave my paperwork to another student and asked her to walk me to my class.

This student looked at the papers to see where to take me and gasped. She said, "You have Miss Tyrant for your teacher? (The name has been changed to protect the not-so-innocent.) She is the meanest teacher in the school!" Not exactly news I wanted to hear. I was already petrified. Hearing that I had unfortunately been placed in the worst possible classroom was not music to my trembling ears.

This student was not mistaken. Miss Tyrant was an ex-army sergeant that never seemed to realize she was now working with young students. There was nothing warm or caring about her; she was very stoic and I think enjoyed seeing us suffer throughout the year. I remember once when she caught a girl in our class chewing gum. The student quickly threw the gum in the trash where it landed in a pile of pencil shavings. Miss Tyrant ordered her to dig the gum out of the shavings and place it back in her mouth. Let's just say she never won the favorite teacher award.

I wanted to run. I knew Indiana was a long way from where I was, but the thought of bolting and heading for "home" was very tempting. That is, until a girl in my class by the name of Susan reached out and wanted to be my friend. She didn't know anything about me, but I'm sure she sensed that this frightened girl from some town out in the boondocks needed a friend. Suddenly I wasn't in this alone. In an instant, I had a cohort. Out of the blue, someone wanted to spend time with me.

From that moment until I left California during my junior year of high school, Susan and I were best friends. We endured school together, we laughed until we cried, and we made weekend trips to the beach together. Susan's smile could light up any room and her friendship was priceless to me.

We stayed in touch for a while after I moved and then finally were able to see each other again in 1984 after the birth of my first daughter. The time together was short but precious. Soon after that, Susan moved and I got wrapped up with raising children and we lost contact. I tried several times to track her down but my attempts failed.

You can imagine my shock then, when one Saturday morning as I was working in my office, I received an e-mail entitled, "Blast from the Past." I opened it up and I couldn't believe my eyes because it was from Susan!

She explained that she had had a vivid dream about me and had told her husband about it. He said she should try to find me, so she went on the Internet, searched my name, and up came my picture along with my first devotional, *Image Seeker*. She wrote that she had immediately begun reading my book and was enjoying getting "caught up" with my life through my writing.

Each word Susan wrote was like music to my ears as I also learned of her family and life in California. It was wonderful to read about her leading devotionals with her nursing staff at the hospital where she worked and the joy she had in spending time with her grandchildren. Her sharing left me wanting to know even more about all the years that had been lost between us.

All I could do was smile from ear to ear and wipe the tears from my eyes. At that moment, I realized how much I had missed our friendship after all these years. Gone were the twenty-nine years that we hadn't had contact, and once again my heart was overflowing with gratitude for this precious "sister" of mine.

This experience has given me just a glimpse of how much it must hurt my Jesus when the connection between Him and me is broken. I can't imagine the pain He must feel when I don't have a desire to spend time with Him, when I let the busyness of life get in the way of our relationship. How convicting it is to me, too, when I realize that at those times, it isn't Him who has moved; it is me. He never leaves me. He never lets other things preoccupy His mind. He never wants anything to come between us or take precedence over our friendship. When the connection between us is broken, it is my fault. It has been my choice.

Are you feeling connected to Jesus today? Is spending time with Him a priority in your life or is He just someone you turn to when you have exhausted all other possibilities? Do you yearn to read His Word, wanting to know everything you can about Him and what He wants for your life? I sure hope so. If not, why not reconnect with Him today? He wants you to realize that you aren't in this world alone and that He desperately wants to spend time with you. The good news is that you won't even have to search for Him on the Internet. He is only a prayer away! I can just about guarantee that the fact that you desire to spend time with Him will make Him smile from ear to ear. And I wouldn't be surprised if He also sheds a tear or two.

My Jesus Prayer

> *Jesus, please forgive me for allowing the busyness of life get in the way of spending time with You. I know that if I'm going to tell others about You, I must spend time basking in Your presence. I love You, Jesus, and want to know everything about You.*

DAY 23

A New Beginning

All praise to God, the Father of our Lord Jesus Christ. It is by his great mercy that we have been born again, because God raised Jesus Christ from the dead. Now we live with great expectation (1 Peter 1:3).

It was a Sunday morning and I was thoroughly enjoying our drive to church. We lived twenty miles from our place of worship and most of our drive was in the country, so there were many signs this particular spring to refresh my soul. How awesome it was to see the brown, drab grass starting to come alive with beautiful shades of green. The winter wheat that had been planted the past fall could be seen pushing its way through the soil. And the best sight of all was what I didn't see: There were no traces of snow.

As I took all of this in that day, the words that kept coming to my mind were *new beginnings*. Winter can feel so very long. It sometimes feels like it is never going to end. I begin to think that the cloudy cold days will always be here and that I will always dread stepping outside, knowing my teeth will be chattering for many miles down the road.

Then, it happens. I have a Sunday morning like this one and I realize that what has been dormant is alive once again and I feel like everything has been given a chance for a new beginning. There is suddenly hope that the sun will shine, the grass will grow, the trees will begin to bud, and (praise be to God!) the temperatures will slowly increase and I will no longer dread stepping outside.

The day our Savior rose from the grave He gave all of us a new beginning that never goes away. At that moment, everything changed. Even though we weren't even born yet, our sins went to the cross with our Lord three days prior and He willingly died with our transgressions on His shoulders.

If He had stayed there, it would have been even worse than a winter that never goes away. Our hope, our chance for a new beginning would have been buried with Him. But He conquered death! He came alive to give us an everlasting hope and a continual opportunity for new beginnings.

Every day gives us that opportunity for a new beginning. No matter what yesterday brought us, today is a new day. No matter what wrong choices we made in the past, we have the choice to grasp a new beginning today. Everything that you and I have done that isn't pleasing to the Lord has already been paid for with His blood. He is just waiting for us to ask for forgiveness and then be willing to take a step into our new beginning.

Where are you today? Is your spirit feeling dormant and lifeless? Do you feel as if there isn't any hope? Look up into the face of your risen King and accept His gift of a new beginning. He has already proven that sin and death cannot overpower Him, so if He already did that, we need to remember that He is *"able, through his mighty power at work within us, to accomplish infinitely more than we might ask or think"* (Ephesians 3:20).

My Jesus Prayer

Jesus, there are times in my life when I need a new beginning. Forgive me for those things that aren't pleasing to You and help me to step out to serve You with renewed power and resolve.

DAY 24

Are You Willing To Tinkle?

So don't make judgments about anyone ahead of time—before the Lord returns. For he will bring our darkest secrets to light and will reveal our private motives. Then God will give to each one whatever praise is due (1 Corinthians 4:5).

I make a point to read through the Bible each year and when I'm reading in the Old Testament I have to be honest, some of it is rather boring. Who begat who (which includes names I can't even pronounce) and what animal could or couldn't be eaten can, at times, cause my mind to wander. But one day I came across a verse that caught my attention and even made me chuckle a little bit.

The verse was Exodus 28:35, *"Aaron will wear this robe whenever he ministers before the Lord, and the bells will tinkle as he goes in and out of the Lord's presence in the Holy Place. If he wears it, he will not die."* I know that I have a weird sense of humor, but I just kept picturing Aaron walking around with his bells tinkling and the scene just made me smile.

Of course, it also made me curious. Why did Aaron have to wear bells when he went into the Lord's presence? Why was it important that he tinkled? These questions took me on a hunt to learn more.

I found out that the bells were worn so that the people knew every move that the priest made while he was in the tabernacle. He was there to perform the sacred rite on their behalf, so the tinkling of his bells was proof to them (even though he was out of their sight) that he was doing just that. This was so important that if the priest failed to wear a robe with the bells, he would be put to death!

This really got my mind wandering. What if you and I had to wear a bell so that we tinkled throughout our day? What if, because we tinkled, everyone would know exactly where we were and what we were doing? Would I be okay with doing that? Would you be okay with doing that?

I guess if we are doing exactly what the Lord wants us to do during our day, we shouldn't mind tinkling. Our day should basically be an open book to those around us and we shouldn't have anything we need to hide. There shouldn't be books we are reading that are filled with pornography or television shows or movies we are watching that take our mind to places not pleasing to the Lord. We should be treating our spouse and our children with the utmost respect and showing love to all those we meet. Our business affairs should be aboveboard with nothing done "under the table" and our employer should see us doing our very best at all times.

I don't know about you, but it made me smile when I read that the priest had to wear the bells. But I have to admit that it would not be nearly as funny if I had to. I like to think that my life is totally focused on my Jesus and His desires for my life, but unfortunately, there are times when I would be ashamed to have others listening to my every word. However, there is Someone who hears my every word and sees my every move. I'm even more ashamed of those times I let Him down and caused Him pain. I'm afraid that I would have been dead a long time ago for not tinkling when I should be.

As we go through our day, let's imagine we have a bell around our neck that others will hear. You may even want to put a bell in your pocket as a constant reminder that there is Someone who knows your every move, hears your every response, and knows your every thought. This just might help us remember that we are to be a light in a very dark world and hopefully, even in the darkness, those around us will hear us tinkle.

My Jesus Prayer

Jesus, help me to always have clean thoughts and motives as I go through my day. Make me mindful that You are ever-present in my life, and the least I can do is be willing to tinkle for You.

DAY 25

Best-Laid Plans

But the Lord's plans stand firm forever; his intentions can never be shaken (Psalm 33:11).

Oh the best-laid plans. This phrase came to my mind at the end of a week in which nothing went as planned. My daughter had asked me if I would be available to go to their home and watch my grandson while they were at work. Their sitter's family was going to be on vacation and so they were in need of my help. I think it may have taken an entire nanosecond for me to answer her. I always wanted to do my very best to be available for them.

Naturally, I could hardly wait for the week to start. I had such plans for my time with them. My grandson and I were going to play and play and then play some more. Since he was at an age when he mimicked just about anything we did, I was going to teach him some new "tricks" that he could show his parents when they arrived home each evening. I even had plans for what I would do while he napped. Yes, I know. Sometimes I'm a little over the top.

Sunday arrived and I excitedly headed for their city. They lived in a second floor apartment, so my son-in-law was always great about coming down and helping me unload my things. Because of this, I texted my daughter as I exited the interstate (yes, I pulled off the side of the road) to let her know that I was close to arriving. I expected an immediate response but it didn't come. Just as I parked outside their complex, I received a text from her saying that I should just come on up because my grandson had just been sick and they were cleaning it up.

That event set the tone for my week. The best-laid plans I had were thrown out the window. Instead of spending my time there playing, I spent my time doing all I could do to help improve his health. He was a very sick little boy. My heart just broke as his precious little face, which was usually filled with smiles, was now pale and tear-streaked. Few nap times were spent in his crib; most of them were spent being cuddled in the rocking chair by this very concerned Grandma.

To make things more worrisome, at 1:30 a.m. on Tuesday, my daughter also became ill. Now not only was there a nine-month-old to care for, but also his mama. Again, plans had to be changed and my time was filled with trying to make both of my patients as comfortable as possible. And yes, not to be outdone, by 1:30 a.m. Friday morning, my son-in-law became ill.

As I went through the week I did everything I knew to do to try to stay healthy. First of all, I hated being sick. Secondly, I knew if I got sick, there wouldn't be anyone to take care of my loved ones that were already ill, and thirdly, I was to speak at a women's retreat on Saturday. I knew that if I was unfortunate enough to become ill with the same side-effects that the others were having, there was no way that I could drive home Friday evening and absolutely no way I could fulfill my speaking engagement.

Each day I held my breath, sometimes literally and figuratively, that I would not come down with this dreaded virus. I think by the end of the week I was actually becoming paranoid that every ache and pain was going to propel me into the land of cooties. But each day I was very thankful that I made it through the hours without debilitating sickness.

By the end of the week the worst was over for my family. They were all regaining their strength, and I was blessed to be able to speak at the Saturday retreat. As I left their place and drove home Friday night, my thoughts were on the amazing God that we serve. It just blew my mind to realize that He was already working on the details of my family's care a couple months before when I was asked to come for that week in February. God knew then that illness was going to invade my family and that they would need someone to care for them.

As I completed my final preparation late Friday night for the Saturday sessions, I had to smile at the irony of the timing of my topic. I had been asked weeks before by those in charge of the retreat to speak on the subject of *Let Go and Let God*. After the week I had just gone through, I wondered why in the world I would still want to hold onto my plans and not let God lead. Why would I be stupid enough to think that my plans were better than His? He has proved to me over and over and over again that He knows every detail of my future and is already working in my tomorrows to make sure whatever happens is in my best interest for today. I would be a fool to want it any other way because the best-laid plans are always His.

My Jesus Prayer

Jesus, why do I ever question Your timing and plans? Thank You for Your patience with me, as I continue to learn that Your ways are always what are best for me. Help me, once again, to put my trust in You and Your best-laid plans.

DAY 26

Confessions From a Cheapskate

And you must love the Lord your God with all your heart, all your soul, and all your strength (Deuteronomy 6:5).

There are very few things that my readers don't know about me, because I tend to be pretty transparent. So you might as well know another tidbit: I'm a cheapskate. I hate to buy anything that isn't on sale. Finding a bargain gets my blood pumping and I use coupons as much as possible. I like to think of myself as being frugal, but that is only because I think it sounds nicer than cheapskate.

When I planted all my flowerpots one spring, I didn't see the necessity in buying new liners for my pots. I had the kind of pots that take a coconut-fiber liner and I thought they still looked adequate for another year, so the planting began. I reasoned that because I had spent more money on the plants than I had planned, this was a place I could cut corners and not have to lay out money for unnecessary liners. I finished them and was thrilled that I could spend the rest of the summer enjoying their beauty. Well, that was my intention.

It didn't take long for the weight of the dirt and the ever-growing flowers to begin to seep through the wall of the liners. Age had taken its toll and what appeared to be strong was really thin and weak. To say I had a mess on my hands is an understatement. Dirt began falling to the ground from the hanging pots as it encircled those already on the ground. I felt almost panicky as I watched my pots fall apart right before my eyes. At that point, I informed my husband that he should never, ever, let me reuse a liner again! Believe me when I say, spending money on new liners each year is well worth every penny when you figure all the time it took me to save those flowers. I won't go into details, but the remedy included duct tape and the result wasn't very pretty! Oh, the hassle I could have avoided if I just wouldn't have gone to such lengths to cut corners to save a little money.

It got me thinking about the times in my life when I have cut corners in my walk with my Jesus. Neglecting my quiet time with Him, choosing to do something for me instead of reaching out to a hurting friend, or doing just the bare necessity to get by in serving Him eventually begins to have an effect on our relationship. It usually isn't noticeable at first, but let the weight of the "dirt" in my life begin to pile up and it isn't long before my weak spots begin to show. People no longer see Jesus when they look at me; instead they see a life that needs more repair than duct tape can cure. Oh, the hassle I could avoid if I just wouldn't go to such lengths to take what appears to be a much easier route.

I need to make sure that I make my relationship with Jesus my top priority by being proactive instead of reactive. Instead of waiting until the crud starts seeping through, I need to make sure my life is "lined" with His truth and power so that others see His beauty in me. Will it cost me more? Yes, it probably will. But in the long run, I think this is one area where not being frugal will be well worth it!

My Jesus Prayer

> *Jesus, help me not to skimp when it comes to serving You. I want to love You with every fiber of my being, no matter what the cost.*

DAY 27
A "Shredding Experience"

And I will forgive their wickedness, and I will never again remember their sins (Hebrews 8:12).

I decided the day had finally arrived. Something needed to be accomplished that should have been done a *very* long time ago. It was time to finally clean out our files in our home office. I am so thankful that I didn't die before I got this done. How embarrassing it would have been to have others go through my things and see that I still had gas receipts from nine years prior. Can you imagine what they would have put on my tombstone? "LuAnn Gerig Fulton, Receipt Hoarder." How tragic that would be!

What a freeing feeling I had as all those unnecessary things from my past were shredded. Some may say that keeping them really wasn't hurting anything, but every time I opened a file drawer a sick feeling came over me. They were a reminder of just one more thing that needed done that I hadn't taken the time to do. I knew these pieces of paper from my past needed to be dealt with and processed; I just needed to make it a priority on my list.

As Dan and I did our marathon shredding (it was just too big a task for one person), I thought about how nice it would be if I could just shred the other things from my past that have cluttered my soul. Those times when I didn't behave as I should or didn't respond to a situation in a way that the Lord would have wanted. I pondered on the many times when I made the choice to sin instead of choosing His way of living. It's not that I haven't confessed those things and asked for forgiveness; I have. But they continue to haunt me and affect me because I haven't forgiven myself.

Do you know that Satan just loves it when we can't forgive ourselves? He makes it a priority to just keep throwing it in our faces, reminding us of all the dirt from our past. He knows he doesn't have to worry about us living a dynamic life for Christ today, as long as he keeps our soul and mind cluttered with the hideous facts of previous days.

One Sunday at our church, a group of brothers and sisters in Christ were brave enough to be real in front of our congregation by participating in "Cardboard Testimonies." If you aren't familiar with these, each person walks out on the platform, carrying a piece of cardboard with words on one side telling what has been a struggle from their past. On the other side, words are written showing the victory they have found in Jesus. It was such a powerful moment. I don't think there were many dry eyes in our sanctuary. I talked with one of the women after the service and she said, "Satan doesn't have anything to hold over me anymore." What an amazing statement! Where Satan once had power, Christ now has victory and control.

Are there things from your past that are still cluttering your soul? If so, make sure that you have confessed them and asked the Lord to forgive you. Once that is done, it becomes your choice if you continue to hold on to the ugliness or whether you will allow it to be shredded. Maybe you need to write down all the things that are keeping you from moving forward in your spiritual walk. Then take that piece of paper and run it through the shredder. Sometimes having the "visual" experience can help free us from those chains that still hold us.

Remember, God can use even the ugliness of our past to bring honor and glory to Him. But we have to be willing to be real and we have to be willing to let go. It's worth making it a priority today.

My Jesus Prayer

> *Jesus, I realize that it will be hard to tell others about You, if I'm still holding onto my past. Help me to let go of those things You have forgiven me for, so that I can freely share Your good news.*

DAY 28

Be Still

Let all that I am wait quietly before God, for my hope is in him. He alone is my rock and my salvation, my fortress where I will not be shaken (Psalm 62:5-6).

I believe that my desire to write stems from the fact that I love to help others with their walk with Jesus. I realize that we are all in this thing called life together, and if I can help others by sharing my life through my words, it will be worth it all.

But I need to be honest with you today. I wrote this particular devotional for me; selfish, huh? The reason is that I was dealing with some issues with my back, which were causing me to have to slow down and behave. Those who know me recognize that I don't do either of those things very well. I love to be busy and able to do things on my own without assistance. In fact, because my daughter knows that I am prone to not behave like I should, she came home for a weekend to be my mother hen. I couldn't make a move without her being right there, making sure I didn't do anything I wasn't supposed to do. At one point she found me walking out to the garden and immediately let me know that that was not allowed! But even though I felt a little "smothered" at times, I also felt very loved and was grateful for her care.

Psalm 37:7a says, *"Be still in the presence of the Lord, and wait patiently for him to act."* Exodus 14:14 reads, *"The Lord himself will fight for you. Just stay calm."* Psalm 46:10a is a verse with which we are all familiar: *"Be still, and know that I am God!"* If Scripture is so clear about the fact that I am to spend time being still and calm, why do I often chafe under it? Is it because I think I know what is best for my life more than He does? Is it because I might realize that I'm not indispensable and that the world will go on if I'm not in the forefront? Or is it because I'm afraid of what

I will hear Him saying if I slow down and really take time to listen to my Jesus?

I do find that when I'm not going full speed through my day, my mind isn't so cluttered. I'm actually able to think about things more clearly, and it gives me better opportunity to listen to the One who so desperately wants to spend more time with me: teaching me, molding me, and just loving me. If I really believe that His ways are just and that His timing is perfect, then I should be at peace with where the Lord has placed me at this time and rest in Him.

I wrote these words for me, but I can't help but wonder if maybe you are also going through a time in your life that wasn't in your plans. Is the Lord asking you to do or not do something that is pushing you way out of your comfort zone? *Be still and let Him work.* I know that it may not be easy, but knowing that you are being obedient to your Jesus will make it worthwhile. We may be amazed at what He can accomplish if we just get out of the way and realize that He is God, and we aren't!

My Jesus Prayer

Jesus, I'm sorry that I often become irritated during the times when I need to be still. Help me learn to surrender and relax, knowing that Your ways and Your timing are perfect.

DAY 29

Connecting to the Power...

But as for me, I will sing about your power. Each morning I will sing with joy about your unfailing love. For you have been my refuge, a place of safety when I am in distress (Psalm 59:16).

I remember the day clearly. It was a Wednesday and it started like most days do for me: up early, exercise, and shower. But then the day changed. Something happened that I feared would affect my entire day. It was an occurrence that I hadn't planned for and could do very little to change. My heart fell; my stomach hurt and to be honest, my mood changed. If you haven't guessed it by now I'll let you in on my tragic event—I discovered our Internet wasn't working.

At this point you may be rolling your eyes, wondering when the men in white coats will finally come and take me away. But for this list-making, highly focused, rather driven computer-aholic, realizing that my connection to cyberspace had been terminated was not a good way to start my day. I already had my hours planned and they were to be comprised of sitting in front of my computer and finishing up a sermon for the following Sunday. I write my own sermons, but the Internet is invaluable for doing research. Yes, I know. Millions of ministers before me wrote a multitude of sermons without any Internet capability and with maybe just a manual typewriter. But my opinion is that if that was what God had wanted for me, He would have had me enter this world thirty years earlier. Yes, I do have a smartphone, which enables me to connect, but its small screen just wasn't going to cut it on that day.

If you haven't shed any tears for me yet, this information just might do the trick. The Internet didn't come back on until 5 p.m.! *Now* you feel my pain, don't you?

Maybe in light of eternity, my Internet going out for over nine hours doesn't rank very high in importance and maybe, just maybe, I overreacted a teensy bit. Unfortunately, just knowing that I didn't have this capability that day almost made me feel panicky. I can't tell you the number of times during those hours that I started to look something up, only to realize, once again, that the words "no connection available" would inevitably pop up on my screen.

I'm sure you will be relieved to know that my sermon did get finished that day even without the aid of the Internet. Looking back, I realize that I was able to get it completed because of another connection to power that I have. This connection *never* goes out, *never* has disrupted power, and *never* makes me see the words "no connection available." This power comes from the Creator of the universe, the One who knows everything about me, all my quirks and idiosyncrasies, and knows exactly what I need when I need it.

With this kind of power available to me seven days a week, twenty-four hours a day, why in the world would there ever be reason for me to panic? If I'm truthful, the only way this power can be disrupted is when *I* make the choice to not be connected. I get busy going full force throughout my day and I neglect to "plug myself in" to the One who can give me the strength, wisdom, and peace that I need to get through my day. My Jesus is never the one to flip the switch off. It is always me and the choices I make that break the connection.

How's your connection? Do you rely on the Internet more than your Jesus? Maybe you're like me and you need to rethink your priorities and fine-tune your focus. I'm so thankful that with my Jesus, I never get a busy signal. I'm never put on hold and I never have to wake up to the news that He has dropped our connection.

Remember, if you feel like the "signal" you are getting from Him is weak, it is *you* that has moved, not Him. Change your direction and start moving toward the power source!

My Jesus Prayer

Jesus, I want my relationship with You to be more important and vital than my relationship with my computer. Help me to stay focused and connected to Your power source so that others will realize from whom I get my strength.

DAY 30
CPR

Publish his glorious deeds among the nations. Tell everyone about the amazing things he does (Psalm 96:3).

I heard a story one day that just seemed unfathomable. A nurse called 911 when a woman in her independent living facility collapsed. The dispatcher informed the nurse that she needed to begin CPR on the woman before the medics could arrive. The nurse refused, saying that it was not their policy to perform CPR in their facility. The dispatcher pleaded with the nurse to find someone, even another resident, who would be willing to begin the CPR that this woman so desperately needed. Again, there was total refusal.

I couldn't believe what I was hearing. This woman had the knowledge and the ability to at least try to save this patient, but because of policies, she made the decision to do nothing. She may have feared losing her job if she went against the company's rules; she may have also feared that if she performed the CPR and caused further injury to the patient, she could be sued.

She had the head knowledge to make a difference, but she wouldn't allow her actions to carry out what she knew. Is that any different than how we as Christians act? We have the head knowledge that each of us will someday be in either heaven or hell, and we know people face death every day. Yet our actions aren't what they should be. We should be telling everyone we meet about our Jesus, that we have the answer to their searching, but we often fail to do so. Is it because we are afraid we may lose some friends if we do? Or is it because we don't want to take a chance of being labeled a Jesus freak or an extremist?

Whatever our excuses are, we shouldn't let them stand in our way of performing CPR. I'm not talking about cardiopulmonary resuscitation. I'm talking about **C**hristians **P**assionately **R**eaching.

Where should we be reaching? First to our Jesus to receive the courage, wisdom, and love that we need to reach out to those that are lost. There are many people who have no clue that Someone died on a cross and then rose three days later so they can spend eternity in heaven. If we don't tell them about our Jesus, who will?

Will they listen? Hopefully. Will they label us fanatics or radicals? Possibly. But I happen to think it's worth the risk. If we really care that there are those who will face eternity in hell if we don't share our knowledge with them, then CPR should be our priority!

My Jesus Prayer

> *Jesus, You have given me the head knowledge to know that everyone will face eternity some day, but I haven't shared that information with all those I meet. Please give me the courage and wisdom to let others know about my precious Jesus and what He has done for them.*

DAY 31
Created in His Image

Thank you for making me so wonderfully complex! Your workmanship is marvelous – how well I know it (Psalm 139:14).

Several years ago, our oldest daughter had all of her wisdom teeth removed and I made the trip to North Carolina to take care of her while she healed. I'm sure she could have survived without my help, but when this Mama has the opportunity to be a mama, I jump at the chance.

After a couple of days of recuperating, Erica said she wanted to get out of the house and do some shopping. At the time, I was in the middle of cleaning her house and had done nothing to myself. I didn't think we were going anywhere so I hadn't taken the time to put makeup on or do much to my hair or appearance.

At this point in the devotional, it is important you know something. After we married, Dan often teased me that I wouldn't even go out to get the mail if I hadn't put makeup on. I have no natural coloring (unless you call pale white a color), so I'm a little scary without makeup. I have relaxed some over the years, so on that day in North Carolina when Erica said she was ready to go, I decided to be wild and go the way I was at that moment. I figured I was a long way from home and wouldn't see anyone I knew, so what would be the harm?

As we walked through the busy store, I looked ahead and saw a woman coming towards us. I didn't know her but immediately I thought to myself, *Wow, I sure wish I looked like her. She is so beautiful and classy looking and really "put together."* Of course, seeing this woman made me feel even worse about myself and embarrassed about how I looked. And then it happened. Much to my horror, as we neared the woman I saw her look at Erica and say, "Hi, Erica, how are you?" What I failed to remember was that even though *I* wouldn't know anyone, my daughter was a schoolteacher and knew many people. She just happened to work with this woman.

To say I wanted to crawl inside the clothes rack is an understatement. Of course, Erica introduced me to her friend, and I'm sure my pallid face was turning beet red about then. As if that wasn't bad enough, we ran into her again at the other end of the store. I was mortified not just for me, but also for Erica, figuring that she was probably not real proud to "show off" her pale mom.

I'm sure Erica grew weary of listening to me replay that scene many times during the rest of the day. I just couldn't stop wondering what that woman must have thought when she saw me. I really wished I would have done even a little something to myself before I ventured out with my daughter.

I returned to Indiana and Erica returned to her teaching job. At the end of her first day back she called me, laughing, and told me that I wasn't going to believe what had happened to her that day. She had seen the woman from the store at school and her first words to Erica had been how much she enjoyed meeting her mom and how beautiful she was. Believe it or not, she was talking about me: pale, white face, and all.

I've thought about this episode in my life many times and it always makes me wonder why I waste time wishing I was someone else. If I just had their hair, figure, complexion, money, self-confidence, or health, my life would be perfect and I could be happy. I fail to remember that I was created to be me and not anyone else. I was created in the image of God and He designed me with exactly what I needed to be who He wanted me to be.

Do you struggle with low self-esteem? Do you waste time whining that you could do so much more for Christ *if* you were more like someone else or *if* you owned something that others have? Allow me to let you in on a secret: That person you wish you were like is probably wishing they were more like someone else! God did not create you to be anyone else but you. Give Him everything you have and allow Him to mold you and make you into the person He knows you can be. That is when you will find true joy and be the most productive for Him.

My Jesus Prayer

> *Jesus, I know that Your Word is true and that Your workmanship is marvelous. Help me to remember that I am Your child and I need to begin acting like one. I was beautifully created in Your image and You don't want me to be anyone else but me.*

LUANN GERIG FULTON

DAY 32

Faith in Action

So you see, faith by itself isn't enough. Unless it produces good deeds, it is dead and useless (James 2:17).

Growing up, there was a story in the Bible that all the kids loved to hear: the story of Zacchaeus. We would hear his story, sing about him and even use hand motions to act it out. Everyone enjoyed talking about the little man who had to climb a tree to see Jesus.

As we know, Zacchaeus was not a favorite among his peers because he was a dreaded tax collector, an employee of the Roman government. Under the Roman system, men bid on the position of tax collector, pledging to raise a certain amount of money. Anything they raised over that amount was their personal profit. Luke says Zacchaeus was a wealthy man, so he must have extorted a great deal from the people and encouraged others to do so as well.

It is surprising then that Zacchaeus was so intent on seeing Jesus. Why would he need Jesus? He probably had everything that the world could give, yet something drew him to the Savior. What is amazing is the fact that all it took was Jesus speaking to him to make him realize the error of his ways. We read in Luke 19:8: *"Meanwhile, Zacchaeus stood before the Lord and said, "I will give half my wealth to the poor, Lord, and if I have cheated people on their taxes, I will give them back four times as much!"*

In those days, if someone was monetarily wronged, the Law required that they be paid back the amount due plus twenty percent (Numbers 5:7, Leviticus 6:5). Zacchaeus was going far beyond what the Lord demanded. He wanted to make sure that Jesus knew he was serious about making a life change. In other words, Zacchaeus demonstrated inward change by his outward action.

How pertinent that is for us today. Following Jesus in our head or heart alone is not enough. Our faith must be shown by changed behavior. If we are a true follower of Christ, it must be obvious to others that we are different, that we want to go beyond what is expected of us in our effort to do His will. It means not finding our self-worth in what the world has given us, but only in what Christ has given us. It means there may be times when we have to take a stand for what the Bible says is true, even when that won't make us popular. We may have times when reaching out to someone others despise may not be the easy choice, but the right choice.

I have two questions for you today. The first one is: *Are you listening?* If Zaccheaus had not been listening to Jesus, he wouldn't have realized his need for change. There is so much noise in our world today that can drown out our Savior's voice if we aren't intentional in allowing Him to speak to us. We must listen to know His plans for us.

The second question is: *Is your faith resulting in action?* It's not enough to just say you are a Christian because, more often than not, your actions will speak much louder than your words to others. Those with whom you come in contact need to see that you are different because of what Christ has done in your life.

I urge you to make it a priority to listen to Christ and then look within yourself. You just may find that there are changes that need to be made so others will see Him in you!

My **Jesus Prayer**

> *Jesus, I know that others won't want to hear about my Jesus, if they don't see my actions living up to my words. Help me, Father, to make the necessary changes in my life so that what I say will be heard.*

DAY 33
God's To-Do List

Trust in the Lord with all your heart; do not depend on your own understanding. Seek his will in all you do, and he will show you which path to take (Proverbs 3:5-6).

He said no. I don't always handle that well. I kept praying and praying, hoping I could get Him to change His mind. But every time His answer was no.

I had been contacted to see if I would serve on a team in the spring for a women's retreat. I love doing things like that, so when the phone call came, my immediate answer was yes. Then I followed my response with the words I knew I better say, "But let me pray about it before I give you my final answer."

That's when I began hearing Jesus' answer and I didn't like it. I kept reminding Him that it was something religious I wanted to do, so I couldn't understand why in the world He wouldn't let me participate. It wasn't like I wanted to spend a weekend bar hopping or gambling my money away. I would do my best to serve Him with whatever job I was given during those days and do it for His glory. But no amount of conniving or trying to make deals with my Jesus made a difference. His answer was still a firm no.

I reluctantly called the woman back and told her that I couldn't serve because Jesus said no. I have learned from experience that the disappointment of having to say no is easier to handle than not following His will for my life. The woman was very understanding and agreed that I needed to listen to His response.

This made me think about the fact that my children didn't always get what they wanted from my husband and me as they were growing up either. They often thought they knew what they needed, but because we were older and more knowledgeable, we knew that what they thought was best, really wasn't the best thing for them. This didn't always go over well with them, and sometimes they felt that pouting was the way to show us their displeasure with our answer. All that usually did was reinforce in our minds that we were right; they weren't ready for the thing they were asking for.

I've heard adults complain that the Lord never answers their prayers, but I often wonder if the problem might be that they aren't listening to Him because they aren't getting the answer they desire. They may be like me and think that they know best, so when His answer isn't what they want to hear, they just quit listening. Prayer is a vital part of our relationship with Jesus, but I think that too often our time is just spent giving Him our "to-do" list. We think He should do this or that, in our timing and with our expected results. When He doesn't answer with the criteria that we have given Him, we say He isn't speaking to us, and let's be honest; we often go off and pout. I have to wonder then if that doesn't just reinforce in the Lord's mind that His answer was correct and we really weren't ready for what we were asking.

I had no clue as to why the Lord told me no but I decided to accept His answer and trust that He knew best. I knew, beyond a shadow of a doubt, that He is much more knowledgeable than me and so maybe what I thought was best, really wasn't the best thing for me. If I wasn't ready for it, I really didn't want it. I would wait for His timing and His will to unfold and trust that His "to-do" list was exactly what I needed!

My Jesus Prayer

Jesus, it's often so hard to accept Your "nos" because I think that I know best. Help me to remember that You know best. Your ways are perfect for me and exactly what I will need for my tomorrows.

LUANN GERIG FULTON

DAY 34

The Rest of the Story

Jesus replied, "You don't understand now what I am doing, but someday you will" (John 13:7).

Yesterday I shared about a time when my Jesus told me no. At the time, it sure didn't make any sense to me. I tried and tried to change His mind but I just kept getting the same response. In the end, I listened and obeyed but I didn't understand His reasoning at the time.

Four months later during the week the retreat would take place, all kinds of issues were going on in my life. In the weeks prior, I had been struggling with a bad sinus infection. My mother-in-law, who I take to all of her appointments, was dealing with a painful foot issue so an additional doctor's appointment had to be scheduled for that week, along with her six-hour treatment for cancer on Friday.

Then, on Wednesday evening, I received a call that my eighty-nine-year-old father had fallen and was being taken to the ER by my brother. He had broken his femur and had to have surgery on Thursday to have three screws put in to stabilize the bone. He was in the hospital for five days.

As I was driving home from the hospital on that Saturday evening, my mind went back to when Christ told me no four months prior. I had no clue what would be going on at that point in my life, but God did. Nothing that was happening had been a surprise to Him. In November He knew that in March there would be other responsibilities that would take my time, and that adding the retreat to my schedule would have meant additional stress. In other words, God knew the rest of the story.

He said no in November so that I could say yes in March to our parents and help them in their time of need. He said no because He loves me enough to want the very best for me. He said no because He is all-knowing and already knew the details of those days in March.

I have to shake my head when I think of the times in my life when I have questioned God's nos. Not once has He ever told me that by mistake or as a way to cause me harm. Every no has been what was best for me at that time and for the days ahead. How amazing it is to know that my heavenly Father loves me enough to tell me no for my own good!

Are you upset today because God is telling you no? Please learn from my mistakes and just accept His answer, knowing that, beyond a shadow of a doubt, it is in your best interest. God always knows the rest of the story and His no just might lead you to a much better yes in the days to come.

My Jesus Prayer

Jesus, I'm so thankful that You can see all my tomorrows and that You love me enough to tell me no. May I always trust Your answers to be for my own good, even when I do not understand them.

LUANN GERIG FULTON

DAY 35
Life is Short

If you forgive those who sin against you, your heavenly Father will forgive you. But if you refuse to forgive others, your Father will not forgive your sins (Matthew 6:14-15).

My memory sure isn't what it used to be. I sometimes wonder if it's because I'm getting older or if my brain is just trying to go in too many different directions. Regardless, I make lots of lists and I love post-it notes, as they help me do my best to stay on top of things.

I am also always on the lookout for anything new that I can use to help me remember what I might easily forget. Some time ago, I came across a picture on the Internet of a wall hanging that was just what I needed to keep our family's birthdates and anniversaries in my eyeshot and in the forefront of my mind. I immediately contacted a friend of mine because I knew she was probably talented enough to make this for me. She did just that and now I am able to see with just a glance who has a birthday and/or anniversary in each month. I have it hanging on the wall in our dining room, and every time I walk by it, it makes me smile.

It not only makes me smile because I love it so; it also makes me smile because it reminds me of how blessed I am by my family. God has been so good to give me a family whom I dearly love. Spending time with them is one of my favorite things to do and I cherish each moment. As our family grows, it doesn't mean that there is less love to go around. It just means that our love grows and expands to a higher level as we welcome each new addition.

Almost sounds like a Norman Rockwell painting, doesn't it? But my life is not a painting. An artist usually takes great pains to make their canvas come alive with a perfect scene with nothing present in it that isn't supposed to be there. The brush strokes are carefully applied to make everything look pristine and flawless. But that isn't reality. The members of my family aren't perfect. None of us are, no matter what "scene" in which we find ourselves. We all have our flaws and we don't always see eye to eye, but our love for each other trumps any differences that we might have.

It breaks my heart when I meet someone and they tell me that they haven't talked to a family member in years. When I ask why, their response is often that something happened in their past that shoved a wedge between them and their relative. Years have gone by and neither side has made the first step towards reconciliation. Pride raises its ugly head, and instead of forgiving and moving on, both sides have dug in their heels and refused to make amends.

1 John 4:20-21 reads, *"If someone says, 'I love God,' but hates a fellow believer, that person is a liar; for if we don't love people we can see, how can we love God, whom we cannot see? And he has given us this command: Those who love God must also love their fellow believers."* For some reason, I think we often read these verses and think that they pertain to just those outside our family, not inside our family. But it refers to both. And unfortunately, I think there are many professing Christians sitting in the pews on Sunday mornings who can love their neighbor but can't love those whom God has placed in their own family.

I sat in the cancer center one Friday with my mother-in-law and I saw it happen once again. A couple came out from seeing the doctor and both of them showed signs on their face that their news had not been good. Then there was a thirty-five-year-old man in the treatment area who talked about how much he and his wife wanted to start a family, but life had thrown them an unexpected curve. Life is short, my friends, and none of us know what event or diagnosis we might experience or receive today. If there is reconciliation that needs to happen in your family, why not be the one to extend your hand to them today? If you wait, it might be too late—and living with regrets is such a waste of your time and energy.

My Jesus Prayer

> *Jesus, I don't want to come to the end of my life and have regrets about fractured relationships in my family. Help me be willing to be the one to extend my hand in forgiveness and heal any broken and hurting wounds.*

DAY 36

He Knew, But He Still Loved

Even before he made the world, God loved us and chose us in Christ to be holy and without fault in his eyes. God decided in advance to adopt us into his own family by bringing us to himself through Jesus Christ. This is what he wanted to do, and it gave him great pleasure (Ephesians 1:4-5).

Let's pretend that I am a senior in high school and an amazing athlete. If you know me well, you know that high school was a very long time ago and the thought of me being an amazing athlete at any stage of my life might end in hysterical laughter. But if you would, please allow me to live in this dream world for a moment.

I am not just an amazing athlete, I am the cream of the crop. Colleges from all over the country are contacting me, wanting me to come to their school and play for their team. I'm getting offers for a free ride with extra perks that only the best can obtain. Everyone showers me with love and attention. They will do just about anything to get me to select their campus.

I finally narrow my choices down and select my college of choice and a meeting is set for me to sign the all-important letter of intent. I arrive at my destination and the room is filled with cameras from every TV station around, making sure that this momentous occasion is captured on film for the world to see. Right before my pen hits the paper though, I lean into the microphone and make the following statement:

"I am honored to be here today and am really excited to play for this team. But before I set foot on this campus to live, I want you know ahead of time that I am not going to follow through on any promises that I make. I know this school has a no drinking policy, but I love to drink and I plan on getting plastered every chance I get. In fact, I'm guessing that I will be hung over so much that I won't make it to most of my classes and I really doubt I will feel up to going to practices. I also know that one of the rules is that guys can't be in the girls' dorm rooms after midnight, but I don't care about that either. I'll have as many guys as I want in my room for as long as I like and you can't tell me any different. I'll run this school down to everyone that I meet and backstabbing others will be a favorite pastime of mine. It won't matter to me how much you plan to do for me; my complete focus will be on me, my needs, and my desires."

By the time I finish my speech, the athletic director is squirming. I'm not the person he thought I was and I'm definitely not someone he wants on the school's team. He stands up, rips up my letter of intent, and says, "Thanks, but no thanks. You're not who we thought you were and we want no association with you." It's interesting that up until this moment, they thought I was pretty amazing and probably about as perfect as they come, but in just a few minutes, their "picture" of me was shattered and their high hopes for my abilities were dashed.

In this pretend scenario, the school only cared about me as long as they thought I was what they wanted for their sports team. As long as I kept up my part of the bargain, everything was fine. But when I showed my faults and my failures, their "love" for me suddenly disappeared.

You are probably wondering where I am going with all of this. This illustration came to my mind as I was thinking about God's love. Did you know that He loved you and me before we were ever born? Notice in our Scripture verse today that He even loved us before the world was created.

This just blows my mind to think that He has always loved me. What really amazes me is that when He decided to love me and adopt me into His family, He knew that I would fail Him. He knew that I would have tons of faults, but that didn't deter Him from loving me.

Nothing I have ever done has surprised Him. When I acted against His teaching; when I chose to sin instead of listening to His leading, not once did He say, "Wow, if I would have known she was going to do that, I sure wouldn't have said I would love her. If I had realized that she wasn't going to live up to my standards, I sure wouldn't have sent My Son to die for her. Thanks, but no thanks, LuAnn. You're not who I thought you were and I want no association with you." He knew, but He still loved. There has been nothing that I have ever done, nothing that I will do today or in the future that will stop Him from loving me.

The same is true for you. God doesn't look on the failures in your past and stamp "rejected" on your life. He knew before the stars were put in place that you would disappoint Him with your actions but that didn't stop Him from loving you then or now. He adopted you knowing full well that you wouldn't be perfect, that you wouldn't live a life free of sin. His love for you was, and continues to be, limitless.

If you struggle with feeling worthy of His love, reread the verses I shared in Ephesians. Remind yourself that God loved you from the beginning, and His choosing to adopt you into His family brought Him great pleasure!

By the way, because we have a God who loves us that much, why in the world wouldn't we desire to love Him? Why wouldn't we do all we could to be a child who acts like Him and loves like Him? No one else even comes close to deserving our praise and our obedience like He does. I hope you feel like I do when I say that there is no other "team" I'd rather be on than His!

My Jesus Prayer

>*Jesus, thank You so much for loving me from the very beginning of time, even with all my faults and failures. I want You to know today how much I love You for all You have done for me.*

LUANN GERIG FULTON

DAY 37

Service or Serve-Us?

For even the Son of Man came not to be served but to serve others and to give his life as a ransom for many (Mark 10:45).

If you are a tech person at all, you probably know about the computerized intelligent personal assistant that is available on many cell phones. I have one on mine and all I have to do is push a button and this computerized assistant asks if it can help me. My primary use of this service is to help me remember to do tasks because my memory leaves something to be desired! I will often ask it to remind me to make a phone call at 9 a.m., send a piece of mail, or even pick something up at a store.

What I find amazing is that if I say thank you to this computerized assistant after it confirms that it will remind me to do a task, it answers me with comments such as, "You're welcome" or, "Just doing my job!" But one day, its response stopped me in my tracks. When I (out of habit) answered with thank you, it said, "I live to serve."

I stood there staring at my phone, looking at those words, and wondered if I could say the same thing about my life. Am I really "living to serve," or am I "living to *be* served"? Am I spelling the word as *service* or *serve-us*? Unfortunately, I think our culture screams at us every day that *we* should be the focus; *we* should demand our rights; *we* deserve to be served. As a result we have a rising number of people who are satisfied to let the government and those around them take care of all of their needs.

But before I point the finger at "those" people, I need to ask myself about me. If I know that I am supposed to reflect Christ's image in everything I do and in every action I make, then I need to begin taking our Scripture in Mark today more seriously. Christ did not come so that He could *get*; He came so He could *give*. Since I am supposed to live as He did, I need to

101

make sure my life is one of service: first to Him, and then to those around me.

I need to ask myself if those I meet are seeing me give whatever it takes to help others. Am I willing to be less comfortable so that others can be more comfortable? Am I willing to use my time and energy to serve others, even if I won't get anything in return? I need to keep reminding myself that people won't want to hear about my Jesus, if they don't feel loved by me first.

Let's make serving others a priority and make sure that we do it with thankful hearts and out of love for our Lord. If He is our focus, then it will be much easier to say, "I live to serve"!

My Jesus Prayer

Jesus, it's so easy for me to be selfish and want my life to be easy and comfortable. Keep me ever mindful that I'm not on this earth for others to serve me, but for me to touch the lives of those You put in my path.

DAY 38

How Bad Is Your Bark?

If you listen to these regulations and faithfully obey them, the Lord your God will keep his covenant of unfailing love with you, as he promised with an oath to your ancestors (Deuteronomy 7:12).

We are the owners of an adorable pug by the name of Olive. Of course, my husband chooses other words to describe her. He says she is one of those dogs that is just so ugly that some find her cute. Regardless, I find her loveable, and that is all that matters!

Olive was the runt of the litter and still only weighs in at fifteen pounds at the ripe old age of eight. But what she lacks in size, she makes up for in personality. If you know anything about pugs, you know that they have to always be the center of attention or they just aren't happy. She is my constant companion and eagerly awaits my sitting down so she can have a lap on which to sleep.

I have often said that I believe Olive is part human, and if I didn't feel that way before, I sure do after what happened one year on her birthday. That morning I told her that if she was a real good girl all day, I would let her have a special treat that evening because it was her special day. She usually only gets this treat on Sunday evenings while we eat our popcorn, and believe me, she knows when it is Sunday! Toward the evening, she gets excited, runs in the kitchen, and goes to the pantry door where the treats are kept. She never does this on any other day than Sunday.

I was so shocked when Friday evening arrived and Olive went to the kitchen, started jumping around, and went to the pantry door. She ran to me and back to the cabinet door and looked back at me. I just had to laugh. She wanted to make sure that I was going to be true to my word by allowing her a yummy delight on her birthday.

When Dan came home that evening from work, I was telling him what had happened and his reply to me was, "If Olive is that smart and understands exactly what you tell her, then she sure is being outright disobedient much of the time." In other words, when I tell her to quit barking (her worst attribute) and she doesn't do it, it isn't because she doesn't understand; she is choosing to be disobedient and would rather I listen to her make noise than come under my authority.

Isn't that just like us? How often does the Lord tell us to do something but we don't comply? Not because we don't understand but because we are choosing to be disobedient. We can put on a good act much of the time and try to look ignorant, but if we are honest, we have to admit that we know what we are supposed to do; we just aren't willing to do it. We would much rather have the Lord listen to us "bark" (by our whining, complaining, and making excuses) than come under His authority.

I just wonder how often we aren't given our "treat" from the Lord at the end of the day because we haven't been obedient. His plans for us are perfect and exactly what we need. He desires to bless us immeasurably. But when we don't come under His authority and do what we are told, we miss out on the showers of blessings that He has waiting for us.

If you find yourself "barking" more to the Lord today than listening, why not work on being quiet in His presence. Allow Him to fill you in on His plans for your life and then comply with His wishes by being obedient. I think you will find that life will be sweeter and less stressful when you allow the Lord to take the lead. As it says in Deuteronomy, if we do our part, He will keep His covenant of unfailing love with us. I ask you: What more could we ask for?

My **Jesus Prayer**

> *Jesus, I don't want to disobey You, but there are times that I do. Please forgive me and help me to learn to be quiet in Your presence as You fill me in on Your plans for my journey.*

DAY 39

If Only...

For he is our God. We are the people he watches over, the flock under his care. If only you would listen to his voice today! (Psalm 95:7).

There had been another school shooting. Just about every TV station, radio station, and newspaper gave a moment-by-moment account of the day. I heard arguing over whether it should be called a tragedy or an atrocity. I heard commentators debate over why people behaved the way they did or what decisions led up to these catastrophic circumstances.

It is not possible for me to think the way some people think. I just don't have it in me. I cannot fathom how someone can deliberately make the choice to kill, injure, and forever change the lives of others. There is no explanation, no commentary, and no psychological evaluation that can get me to understand those thought patterns. A person whose mind is so bent on evil makes decisions that most of us just can't grasp.

If only someone could have intervened. *If only* someone could have said something to those with such malicious hearts that would have changed their minds and their plans. *If only* their parents would have raised them differently. *If only* their teachers would have spent more time teaching them one-on-one. *If only*....

We can spend hour after hour listing the *"if only"* scenarios, but it doesn't change what has happened in the past. We can't go back. Yesterday has already been documented in the record books and nothing we can do can change that.

Today—this twenty-four-hour period—is the only segment of time in which we can do something to make a difference. Unfortunately, the only part of today that we have jurisdiction over is ourselves. We can change no one. We cannot make anyone think the way we think, behave the way we think they should behave, or make decisions that we think should be made. We only have the ability to change us.

That stinks, doesn't it? It's so much easier to spend our time wishing everyone else would change. The world would be a much better place if *they* would just get their act together. I mean, I have reasons for why I behave the way I do. *If only* you knew what I have been through, you would surely understand.

The sobering thought is that others' lives may never change if they don't see a change in us. If we aren't living lives that are completely sold out to Christ, lives that are filled with His Spirit and controlled by His touch, they may never know that we have the answers to their pain and hurt.

In light of tragic events such as this, I think there is only one *"if only"* we should be thinking about: *If only* they could have met my Jesus and realized the sacrifice that had already been made for them. So true. But *they* may never meet my Jesus if they don't see Him in me.

No matter how each incident is labeled or described, it comes down to the fact that we have a world that needs Jesus. The question is: *Are you willing to be Jesus with skin on today so others will have hope for their tomorrow*? Just think, *if only* you would change, they could see Jesus!

My Jesus Prayer

Jesus, I know that there are changes that I need to make in my life, so others will want to hear about my Jesus. Mold me, shape me, and conform me to Your will is my prayer.

DAY 40
Italian Broccoli

> *Beware of false prophets who come disguised as harmless sheep but are really vicious wolves. You can identify them by their fruit, that is, by the way they act. Can you pick grapes from thornbushes, or figs from thistles? A good tree produces good fruit, and a bad tree produces bad fruit* (Matthew 7:15-17).

Every spring when we decide what we will raise in our garden, I like to find something new to plant that I have never had before. I was so excited one year when I found something I had never even heard of: Italian broccoli. The picture on the seed package caught my attention because it didn't look anything like the broccoli in our stores. It's a lighter color, shaped differently, and just has an intriguing look.

I was excited to get the seeds in the ground and then anxiously waited for them to peek through the soil. It didn't disappoint me. Within a few weeks it made its appearance and I was thrilled. (I know, it doesn't take much to make me happy). Throughout the summer we watched the beautiful plants grow higher and higher and higher. Others who saw it commented on how nice the plants were and that we should have plenty of broccoli to enjoy. Well, so we thought.

While others were harvesting their delectable American broccoli from their garden, we were trying to patiently wait for some sign of an Italian vegetable. Every week I checked the tall plants, growing over waist high, hoping to see something beginning to form and every week I was disappointed. The vegetation looked like broccoli plants; but it just never produced.

I was thinking about how this situation is similar to some Christians today. For all intents and purposes, they look like Christians. People observing their lives as they go to church every Sunday morning and maybe even Sunday night believe their life is where it should be. They even have a fish sign on the back of their car and religious pictures on the walls of their homes. They may even be well known and spend time preaching from a pulpit, but unfortunately, that's where it ends. They may "look" like a Christian, but if a person observes them closely, there isn't any fruit. Their relationship with Christ is more of a convenience, lacking depth and real fruit.

Scripture warns us to be careful and to look closely at those who profess to be followers of Christ. There were false teachers in biblical times and there are false teachers today. We must be intentional in making sure that our lives are not only producing fruit, but that those who we listen to and follow are glorifying Christ, and not themselves.

Others will be recognized by their fruit and so will we. How do you measure up? Is your attendance in church on Sunday mornings your only sign of being a Christian or are others seeing your "fruit" during the week? Just as I was disappointed in not seeing any broccoli on my plants, I don't want Christ to be disappointed in me when He sees what I haven't produced. It doesn't matter how "Christian" I might look, if my life isn't displaying the work that has been done in me by Christ to others, my witness will be of no avail.

My prayer is that others will recognize you and me by our fruit, not for our glory, but for His. Will you join me in being intentional in not concentrating on our appearance but on our production instead?

My Jesus Prayer

Jesus, I never want anyone to look at me and not see any fruit. Help me not to just "look" like a Christian on the outside, but be filled to the brim and overflowing with Your Spirit on the inside. Then, and only then, will my fruit begin to show to those around me.

DAY 41
Just Not Feeling It...

For I know the plans I have for you, says the Lord. They are plans for good and not for disaster, to give you a future and a hope (Jeremiah 29:11).

When our children were growing up, it wasn't uncommon to hear a certain statement come from their mouths. I would tell them to do a chore, such as cleaning their bedroom so the floor was visible, and I would receive this response, "But I don't *feel* like cleaning my room." To which I would usually reply, "Well, if I only did what I *felt* like doing, not much would get done." If that comment didn't tug at their heartstrings and they still didn't want to obey, I would tell them that if they didn't do what they were told to do, they would be *feeling* something warm on their backsides.

I can laugh at those times now, but when I was in that situation, I usually wasn't doing much laughing. I just wanted them to do what I wanted them to do without arguing. Was that too much to ask? It frustrated me when they couldn't comprehend the fact that life would be much happier for all of us if they would just trust me to know what was best for them. From my perspective, it didn't matter whether they *felt* like doing something or not! If I, as their parent, wanted them to dust the furniture, then they should cheerfully bow to me and say, "Yes, dear mother, your wish is our command." Okay, maybe I was expecting a little too much.

Reliving those days makes me ask myself if my heavenly Father ever tells me to do something only to hear me say, "But I don't *feel* like doing that." If I am honest, I have to say yes, He has heard that response from me. I wonder if He gets frustrated when I don't comprehend the fact that life would go much easier if I would just trust Him to know what is best for me. I know there have been many times when my disobedience deserved a good "warming of my backside" and that could have been avoided if I would have just done what I was told to do.

Is your heavenly Father asking you to do something now that you don't *feel* like doing? Are you listing reason after reason why you don't think you should have to obey Him? When you do this, you are actually telling Him that you know more than He does. There usually isn't a good outcome when a child feels that way about their parent—especially when the parent is the God of the universe. It might be something as simple as going to church on Sunday. You know He wants you to put aside that time to worship Him, but because you don't *feel* like going you find every excuse as to why you can't fit that in your schedule. Or maybe He is asking you to step out of your comfort zone and tell an unsaved friend about your Jesus. But because you fear looking "different" or being called a religious freak, you *choose* to be disobedient.

As you go through your day today, be intentional about obeying your Father, whether you *feel* like it or not. I am confident that you will be blessed for your obedience, and you may be surprised that your *feelings* just might change as you do what He is telling you to do. He died for us and rose again so we can have a future with hope, and all He asks of us in return is to trust Him and be obedient. Is that too much to ask?

My Jesus Prayer

Jesus, help my feelings to not get in the way of obeying and trusting You. I know that Your plans are good and are exactly what I need at this time, so help me to do whatever You ask of me.

DAY 42

Life Stinks

Dear friends, don't be surprised at the fiery trials you are going through, as if something strange were happening to you. Instead, be very glad – for these trials make you partners with Christ in his suffering, so that you will have the wonderful joy of seeing his glory when it is revealed to all the world (1 Peter 4:12-13).

Let's be honest. Life stinks sometimes, doesn't it? In fact, I'm sure many of us have had seasons of our lives when we have wondered if the "smell" would ever go away, or if we would always have to live with pain and difficulty.

Why does a loving God make us go through trials and tribulations? Why can't He just pave a smooth road on which we can travel? Doesn't He realize that we could be a better witness for Him if we didn't have any problems or temptations? Why, people would flock to church if they knew that all of their problems would go away if they just followed Christ!

Unfortunately, I have spent many an hour asking the Lord to remove difficulties from my life. I've asked, begged, even pleaded at times for Him to make my life easier and more problem-free. That is probably why a statement I heard one time hit me between the eyes.

I was listening to a sermon once, minding my own business, when all of a sudden I heard the speaker say, "Do you pray more to be developed or delivered?" *Ouch.* That hurt. Yes, I've prayed for Him to develop me into the Christian He wants me to be, but I usually want to be delivered from my difficulties more. It's kind of like when I've prayed for Him to give me patience but I wanted Him to give it to me right now!

It is important that we grasp the fact that the Lord is more concerned about what is happening *in* us, than what is happening *to* us. He wants to see us growing in our faith and in our trust, *in spite of* our circumstances. He wants us to rely on Him completely in the good times and the bad, knowing that He only wants the very best for us. He wants every situation, every trial, and every temptation to make us look more like Him, but more importantly, He desires that *we* also want every situation, every trial, and every temptation to make us look more like Him. If that is what we really long for, then how we see our trials and difficulties will change. It will be at that point when we will begin to focus more on our development than on our deliverance.

Is your life pretty "smelly" right now? Begin to focus on asking the Lord to develop you during this time so you will look more like Him, instead of asking for the difficulties to go away. I'm thinking that if we do this we just might begin to see the "stink" as a positive instead of a negative. I don't know how you feel, but trading in my looks for His sounds like a pretty good deal to me.

My Jesus Prayer

Jesus, I can't imagine being glad when I am suffering but I know these times will be worth it if they make me look more like You. Help me to use these times of difficulty to show others Your power and strength.

DAY 43
Light Bulb Moments

For the word of God is alive and powerful. It is sharper than the sharpest two-edged sword, cutting between soul and spirit, between joint and marrow. It exposes our innermost thoughts and desires (Hebrews 4:12).

I love what I call a light bulb moment. It's that moment when something you read or have heard begins to make sense. It's as if a light bulb comes on in your brain and you learn information you didn't know before, or something you didn't understand suddenly makes sense.

As a writer and speaker, I believe my responsibility is to impart what I have written and what I say in such a way that my readers and listeners have these kinds of moments. I am to convey what God has laid on my heart so that everyone can understand the points I am making. I am passionate about what I share and I desperately want to convey my thoughts in a way that makes you want to be passionate about them too. Believe me, especially in the pulpit, it is usually fairly simple to see who is understanding and absorbing what I am saying and who has either tuned me out, or even worse, decided to take their morning snooze.

But if a person doesn't read what I have written or make a point to listen to me, they aren't going to understand what I am trying to convey and there is no way they will have a light bulb moment. Even if they own my books, receive my weekly devotional, or sit in a sanctuary where I am delivering the morning message, they will learn nothing if they don't either read it or listen. They must choose to do this. It is impossible to learn through osmosis; action has to be taken.

I was thinking about this one day as I was talking to a friend and I had a light bulb moment. It suddenly occurred to me that as difficult as it is for me to witness through my ministry when others won't read or listen, it is that much more difficult for our Savior to get through to us when we neglect to read His Word and listen to His voice. I often hear people say that they just don't know what they are supposed to do. They're frustrated, lost, and confused and really want some direction in their life. But when they are asked if they are reading their Bible and spending time in prayer their answer is usually no. Oh, they own a Bible and they sit in a sanctuary every Sunday, but effort is not made to open His Word and really listen to His servant share from the pulpit.

How that must bring pain to our Lord. He loves you and wants so much more for you. But for you to fully comprehend how much He cares for you, to fully grasp the magnitude of what He has done for you, and to fully realize where He wants to lead you in the days ahead, you have to take action. You have to open His Word and listen to His voice. It's impossible to have any light bulb moments if you aren't intentional in getting to know Him.

Have you lost your way and aren't sure what path to take?

> *"Your word is a lamp to guide my feet and a light for my path"* (Psalm 119:105).

Do you have a feeling of hopelessness?

> *"You are my refuge and my shield; your word is my source of hope"* (Psalm 119:114).

Do you feel like the Bible is too hard to comprehend?

> *"The teaching of your word gives light, so even the simple can understand"* (Psalm 119:130).

Do you feel like Christ's words really weren't meant for you?

> *"My child, listen to me and do as I say, and you will have a long, good life. I will teach you wisdom's ways and lead you in straight paths"* (Proverbs 4:10-11).

Is that a glow I see in your head? I sure hope so, because there isn't anything much better than a light bulb moment!

My Jesus Prayer

> *Jesus, forgive me for those times when I have failed to open up Your Word to let it speak to me. I know that I can't be a light in this world if the "fuel" of Your words isn't within me. Teach me Your ways, oh, Lord.*

DAY 44
Living Life As A Worrywart

Don't worry about anything; instead, pray about everything. Tell God what you need, and thank him for all he has done. Then you will experience God's peace, which exceeds anything we can understand. His peace will guard your hearts and minds as you live in Christ Jesus (Philippians 4:6-7).

My sermon title was "Living Life as a Worrywart." I won't bore you with my entire sermon, but it did have a few noteworthy points. If we look at worrying realistically, we know three things:

1. Worrying is *unreasonable.* Most of us know deep down that worrying isn't going to change the situation. You cannot worry enough to change anything. Matthew 6:27 says, *"Can all your worries add a single moment to your life?"* Of course, they can't! But I bet if we worry we can *deduct* some hours from our lives.

2. Worrying is *unhealthy.* I've never had a doctor tell me, "LuAnn, you need to worry more. It would be so good for your health if you just stewed more about your problems." Proverbs 12:25 tells us, *"Worry weighs a person down; an encouraging words cheers a person up."* I have heard doctors say that many of the health problems they see on a daily basis aren't really physical problems, but emotional ones that have, over time, caused physical problems.

3. Worrying is *not* biblical. I couldn't find any scripture in the Bible that instructed me to worry. There wasn't any verse that said, "If your son or daughter is going through something that is difficult, *then* you can worry." Or, "Don't worry, *unless* you lose your job. Then you have the right to worry." There were no scriptures telling me to worry anywhere in any circumstance. However, the Bible has a lot to say about why I *shouldn't* worry, and today's scripture in Philippians is a great one on which to meditate.

First Peter 5:7 tells us that we are to *"Give all your worries and cares to God, for he cares about you."* Notice it says we are to cast *all* of our worries and cares on Him. The problem is that most of us do our casting like we do when fishing. We cast our worries and anxieties out, and then we reel them back in. We need to cast them all on Him and then leave them there.

Is your stomach in knots because you are so worried? Are you missing out on life today because you are so stressed about your tomorrow? If you answered yes to either of those questions, you are probably a worrywart like me. Instead of worrying today, let's practice "casting" our cares on our Jesus. But don't forget, we need to leave the "reeling" to Him!

My Jesus Prayer

> *Jesus, You know that this is an area where I struggle.*
> *Help me to cast all of my worries on You and let You*
> *handle them. Help me to keep in mind that others*
> *won't want to hear about You if they see I can't trust*
> *You with everything in my life.*

DAY 45

Loving Forever

The Lord says, "I will rescue those who love me. I will protect those who trust in my name. When they call on me, I will answer; I will be with them in trouble. I will rescue and honor them" (Psalm 91:14-15).

On October 3, 2012, Dan and I celebrated thirty-one years of marriage. We gave each other cards that morning, and even though we bought them at different stores, we had purchased the exact same card. Why? Because it said what both of us were feeling after all these years. The front of the card said, *"I'll Love You Forever"* and the inside talked about the fact that we have seen each other through our best and worst and everything in between. It's so true! We have laughed together and cried together and neither of us can imagine life without the other.

The week leading up to this anniversary had been one of the "worst" times, because for the umpteenth time in our marriage, I had been very ill. Once again, Dan showed me how much he loved me, not just by saying the words, but by his actions. He tenderly cared for me, making me as comfortable as possible. I could even see in his eyes that, if he could, he would take the pain from me. This is what marriage is all about: loving your spouse forever, even in the times when they are unlovable, and in my case, looked like death warmed over.

We made the decision on Oct. 3, 1981 that no matter what came our way, Christ would be the Head of our home, the center of our marriage, and the word "divorce" would not be in our vocabulary. Has it always been easy? No, it hasn't. We have most definitely seen the best and the worst. There were times when the easy thing to do might have been to walk away and turn our backs on the vows we had spoken.

Making your marriage work is not easy and we often think that the grass looks much greener in another location or with another mate. What we often fail to remember is that whatever grass we are on needs watered, so it is important that we put our effort into tending to the place where we have been planted. We found that even when we thought we couldn't go on, Christ was there to hold us together until the sun shone again.

You may be facing a marriage that is falling apart, a health situation that doesn't make any sense, or a financial crisis that has you scared to death. Whatever it is, make the choice to put Jesus at the center of your life and make the vow to love Him forever. The road may not be easy, but I guarantee that it will be easier with Him holding your hand every step of the way!

My Jesus Prayer

> *Jesus, it often seems easier to run than to stay and work on the issues I am facing. Help me to run toward You in those times, grasping Your hand which will lead me through the valley and into the sunlight.*

DAY 46

Moving Mountains

"You don't have enough faith," Jesus told them. "I tell you the truth, if you had faith even as small as a mustard seed, you could say to this mountain, 'Move from here to there,' and it would move. Nothing would be impossible" (Matthew 17:20).

Do you ever question if your prayers are getting through? Wouldn't it be nice if, after we prayed, we would receive an e-mail, stating "Prayer delivered"? Then we would know beyond a shadow of a doubt that God was listening to our requests.

I believe God understands the doubts that we sometimes have and occasionally answers a prayer immediately just to confirm in our minds that He is alive and well and always listening. I witnessed this happen a few years ago.

I was teaching a discipleship class for women in our community and as usual, we ended our time together in prayer. One of our members was unable to attend because she was home getting ready for guests to arrive for the weekend. During our time of prayer, one of the ladies prayed for this member that God would touch her in a very powerful way. When we ended our meeting, I checked my phone and realized I had a text message from this woman for whom we had just prayed.

She was asking for prayer because her ankle and foot were really hurting her and she had been unable to do many of her tasks that evening. She was frustrated, in a great deal of pain, and just felt overwhelmed. I informed the group of her text and was glad that she had just been prayed for by one of the ladies.

The next morning, this woman contacted me and said that the strangest thing had happened the night before. She said that after she had sent her text, she immediately began to feel warmth in her ankle and foot. The pain instantly began to subside and by that next morning there was no pain at all. I checked the time her text was sent, and it was right at the time when the woman prayed for her.

Coincidence? Absolutely not! Our God is alive and well and powerful. He allowed us to be a part of an amazing miracle that evening. He can use us, with all of our faults and failures, to touch the lives of those who are hurting physically, mentally, and emotionally. He just asks that we put our faith and trust in Him and allow Him to work as only *He* can.

I love what Paul said in Romans 1:8, *"Let me say first that I thank my God through Jesus Christ for all of you, because your faith in him is being talked about all over the world."* That's the kind of faith I want. Faith that is talked about all over the world. Will you join me? Let's ask God to move mountains today and then see what He will accomplish through us!

My Jesus Prayer

Jesus, I am excited to see what You can accomplish through me today. Help me to be mindful of Your presence as together we move the mountains before us!

DAY 47

Pruning Petunias

"Yes, I am the vine; you are the branches. Those who remain in me, and I in them, will produce much fruit. For apart from me you can do nothing" (John 15:5).

I love summer. I love the warmth, the sun, the green grass, and not having to wear a coat to go outside. Most of all, I thoroughly enjoy working in my flowerbeds, of which I have several. One of my preferred flowers is the petunia. It comes in a variety of colors and, if cared for correctly, will bloom profusely for several months.

Unfortunately, if my petunias are left to take care of themselves, it doesn't take long for them to begin looking bad. The key to their health is receiving plenty of water, fertilizer, and lots of pruning. I do my best to go over them every day, pulling off any despairing-looking blooms so that only the vibrant, healthy-looking flowers are left. If I skip a day there are, naturally, more dead flowers to contend with and if I miss several days, it can seem an almost overwhelming task to get them back to their beautiful state.

As I was working one day in my gardens I was thinking about how much those petunias are like me. As long as I am spending time with the Lord, the Master Pruner, each day, my life can be full of blossoms and growth. If I miss a day with Him, those things (sins) that are ugly in my life start to distract from my beauty. And with each day that I miss, more of my unattractive qualities are evident and, unfortunately, it doesn't take long for others to miss seeing His image in me because my ugliness has won out.

If I want the privilege of telling others about my Jesus, I need to make sure I am well pruned. That pruning doesn't always feel good, but if I want new growth in me, I have to be willing to come under His knife.

Just like my petunias, I also need to make sure that I am receiving fertilizer to help me grow. The Bible is meant to give me the nutrients and growth that I need to have a vibrant, personal relationship with my Jesus. I am the only one who can make sure I'm spending time learning from His Word. No one else can do it for me. I can't just depend on my pastor to hear from Jesus, hoping he or she will tell me from the pulpit what I need to know. It is my responsibility to make sure my spiritual life is being watered and fertilized each and every day.

As you are enjoying this day that the Lord has given us, keep your eyes out for petunias. Let them be a constant reminder that you need to be pruned daily so that you will reflect His image. If you make that a priority, you will surely be a beautiful display of His handiwork!

My Jesus Prayer

> *Jesus, I know that it sometimes causes me pain when You have to prune me, but it is necessary if I want to grow in You. Thank You for loving me enough to want me to be who You intended me to be: a beautiful display of Your handiwork!*

DAY 48
Pride and My Big Mouth

Pride goes before destruction, and haughtiness before a fall (Proverbs 16:18).

I am sure that many of you are familiar with our scripture today in Proverbs. I think I could reword this to say, "Pride goes before I open up my big mouth." As you can see, my version is much more blunt!

Oh, how I wish I hadn't learned this verse the hard way! Let me give you an example. Ever since I was married I have taken pride in my home. I have done my best to make sure that it was fairly in order and that it was a place where others felt warm and welcomed. I don't think there is anything wrong with this kind of pride. I believe that God wants us to take care of what He has given us and then use it for His glory.

Where I have gotten into trouble is when the pride that I have felt has turned into pride in what I can accomplish. Through the years, if I heard that someone had a cleaning service for their home, my response was always, "Well, I will never do that. The day that I can't clean my own home will be a pretty sorry day. Plus it would never work because I would have to clean my house before the cleaning service came, because I wouldn't want them to see my dirt."

I stayed true to this haughty declaration until all of our kids were grown and we were left with an empty nest. Yes, there was less to clean with only two adults living in the house, but the fact that I've had four back surgeries began to work into the equation. I was now left to do most of the cleaning myself and I was finding it harder and harder to keep things the way I liked them. When my husband asked if I needed help, my response was always a resounding *no,* I could handle it on my own.

I will never forget the day when the Lord dealt with me on this issue. We have a walk-in shower and I could only clean one panel before the pain in my neck and shoulder reared its ugly head and I had to stop. I would then wait several days until the pain subsided to do the next panel. On this particular day, as I was scrubbing one of the panels, I was also questioning the Lord. *Why in the world do I have to be in this much pain just washing a stupid shower? Lord, I have so much to do in my ministry, which I know beyond a shadow of a doubt that You have called me to, and yet I have to deal with this pain when I am accomplishing my day-to-day responsibilities. Why can't You just heal me so that I can get the things done that I need to do?*

I heard Him whisper in my ear, "LuAnn, what are you willing to give up to serve Me? How much of your pride are you willing to swallow, so you can do what I have called you to do? When will you be willing to admit that you need help?" That's when I realized that instead of finding my identity in Christ, I was finding my identity in what I could do on my own. As stupid as it sounds, I was holding on to my pride in what I could accomplish by cleaning my own home, instead of what He could accomplish through me.

The day when two women walked into my home to clean, I cried. I'm sure they thought they had just entered the home of a mentally unstable person, but letting go of what I had held onto with white knuckles was not easy. I struggled as a part of me still felt like a failure for not being able to do everything on my own.

Every two weeks they showed up to eradicate my house of the dirt. Turning my home over to them got easier and, if I'm honest, it was wonderful to have the entire house clean all at one time. Their help allowed me more time to do the things that the Lord called me to do.

How are you doing with your pride? Is there something that you are holding onto because of how it makes you feel, even if it isn't what God wants? Maybe it is a good thing that you are clinging to. Maybe it is a position or responsibility in the church that you have held onto for many years and you know God is telling you that it's time to allow someone else to do it. But it has been your "baby" and you feel you are the only one that can do it right and so your pride is getting in the way of your obedience. Maybe it is in a more personal area of your life. Maybe there is conflict between you and someone else and you know that you should swallow your pride, go to them, and ask for forgiveness. Instead, you dig your heels in and wait for them to make the first move. Or, maybe God is asking you to change careers, leaving a prestigious job that brings you lots of recognition and pats on the back for a behind-the-scenes job that won't attract much attention.

Whatever it is that you are holding onto that is feeding and fueling your pride, why not turn it over to the Lord? You just might discover that what He is asking you to give up may not be nearly as wonderful as what He has in store for you. He has proven to me over and over again that His ways are perfect and exactly what I need to become more like Him, which should be our goal. Whether we are cleaning toilets, working in a factory, running a corporation, retired, or writing a devotional, our focus should be on seeking His image for our lives. Then others won't see us when they are in our presence; they will see Jesus. In my case, I know looking at Jesus will be much more pleasant than looking at my big mouth!

My Jesus Prayer

Jesus, why do I hold onto things that have no eternal consequence? Please help me loosen my grip on what You desire for me to give up. I know that only then will I begin to look more like You as I follow Your perfect ways.

DAY 49

Priorities

You must worship no other gods, for the Lord, whose very name is Jealous, is a God who is jealous about his relationship with you (Exodus 34:14).

Have you ever had a day that just dragged on and on? A day when you thought for sure it had to be at least 2:00 p.m. but when you checked the clock, realized it was only 10:00 a.m. and you felt like crying? I have. But to be honest, I have more days that just seem to fly by. Days when if I just had a couple more hours to work on my to-do list, I just might get caught up. The truth is, though, if I were given those extra couple of hours, I probably wouldn't have the energy to do more work anyway!

The question becomes, "Is what I'm spending my day doing making a difference in the light of eternity, or is it just busywork?" I can find many worthwhile tasks to fill my day, but are they duties that the Lord has prescribed, or are they the things that I want to do?

Many years ago I heard a statement that spoke to me. I jotted it down and it has been beside my bed ever since. The statement was, "What you prioritize is what you will eventually worship." If you asked me what or whom I worship, my immediate answer would be that, of course, I worship my Jesus. I'm surely not like those people I read about in the Old Testament who just kept returning to their idols. How could they be so stupid to bow down to their man-made statues? Isaiah 2:8 sums up what they were doing: *"Their land is full of idols; the people worship things they have made with their own hands."* It is obvious that they had lost their way; they were more concerned about what they were doing and what they had achieved than what God had done and what He wanted to accomplish within and through them.

I'm so glad I'm not like them—or am I? When my life is spiraling out of control and I feel overwhelmed, could it be that I feel that way because my priorities have gotten out of whack? Could it be that my agenda has become the idol that I'm worshipping and I have left God out of the picture?

Life can become hectic as it fills up with job responsibilities, ballgames, barbecues, as well as school and church responsibilities. None of these things are bad, but we need to be intentional to make sure they don't become our priority. What message are we sending our children when we make the decision that going to the lake or attending the ballgame on Sunday is more important than worshipping with our brothers and sisters in Christ? What message are our friends receiving when they hear us say that we don't have to go to church on Sunday because we choose to worship God as we are out in nature; it's just not necessary to go into a church to give praise to our God?

I pray that your days will be filled with all those activities that make you feel fulfilled. However, I also pray that you won't forget who should be the center of your attention as you go through each day. Allow your Jesus to lead, guide, and prioritize your day. If you do that, you will be able to look back on days gone by, knowing that what you accomplished *did* make a difference in the light of eternity. I just can't think of a better way to spend our days.

My Jesus Prayer

Jesus, it is so easy for me to fall into the trap of focusing on my agenda instead of Yours. Help me to remember today that every choice I make should be from Your leading and direction.

DAY 50
So Big!

For the Lord your God is the God of gods and Lord of lords. He is the great God, the mighty and awesome God (Deuteronomy 10:17a).

When our kids were small, we used to ask them how big they were. We would say to our son, "How big is Adam?" He would put his little arms straight up in the air and then we would say, "*So* big!" It was one of those fun games we played that usually brought a big smile to our little one's face.

Today I want to play that game with you, but with a slightly different slant. I want to ask you, not how big *you* are (because if you are like me, the answer would be a little embarrassing!) but how big do you see your God? Is He only big enough to handle *some* of your problems? Do you only turn to Him in a time of emergency?

The reason I am asking this today is because I often hear Christians talking about their problems as if there were no hope; as if what will be, will be, and nothing or no one could make a difference. They talk with such despair, lamenting about the doom and gloom of their days ahead. It makes me wonder what others, especially non-Christians, are thinking. If I was not saved and I heard a professing follower of Jesus moaning and whining about their situation, I doubt I would want what they have. If their Jesus, with whom they claimed to have a personal relationship, wasn't powerful enough to handle *their* problems, there would be no reason for me to think He could handle mine.

I think sometimes we use the negatives in our lives as an excuse for why we aren't doing more for our Jesus. There are a litany of excuses: "If you just knew how I was raised, you would understand why I can't do more for Jesus. If you knew about the terrible job I have, you would agree that

I have a right to feel sorry for myself." Until we realize that we cannot blame others or our circumstances for the status of our relationship with Jesus, we will never see Him for the mighty, powerful God that He is and wants to be in our lives.

I wonder what we are missing out on when we don't allow God to handle any and all the situations of our lives. What misery could be avoided if, when difficulties or concerns arose, we immediately gave it over to Him and let Him take complete control of our lives? Would we have fewer ulcers? Would we retain more hair on our head? Most importantly, would we be a better example of God's power and grace to those with whom we come in contact?

The next time anyone asks you how big your God is, I hope you will get a huge smile on your face, raise your arms over your head, stand way up on your tippy toes, and say, "So big!" Then prove it by the way you live!

My Jesus Prayer

Jesus, I miss out on so much in my life because I forget how big and powerful You are. Help me not to dwell on the size of my problems, but on the size of my Jesus, because there is nothing in my life that You can't handle.

DAY 51

Resolutions

For we are God's masterpiece. He has created us anew in Christ Jesus, so we can do the good things he planned for us long ago (Ephesians 2:10).

I am artistically challenged. Just hearing the word "art" makes me feel a little queasy. I remember when I was in school and they required us to take an art class. I would have rather cleaned the toilets with a toothbrush than take that class. I'm not sure I will ever forget the day they told us we were going to make a pinch pot out of clay. All I could think was, *seriously*? How in the world was that going to help me in my future? It was just torture, pure torture for me.

I think one of the reasons that I don't enjoy art is because I'm not a very patient person. I want things done and I want them done now, and creativity often takes time that I'm not willing to give. I wish I could take that lump of clay and make something beautiful out of it; but if I'm honest, I'm just not willing to put the time and effort into making it become a reality.

I was thinking recently about the fact that not only am I artistically challenged, but I'm sometimes challenged in being a Christian too. I know how I should be living and what I should be doing, but I think about how much effort and time it is going to take to be the person God wants me to be, and I give up before something beautiful can be created in my life. It's often easier to do nothing and just be content with the status quo than to push out of my comfort zone and allow God to create a masterpiece within me.

Fear often plays a part in my choice to not want God to work in my life too. What will He ask me to do? What will others think of me if I am more vocal about my beliefs and values? What if I'm put in a situation where

ASK ME ABOUT MY JESUS

I speak out and I find myself standing alone? I've been there in the past, and I know it isn't a very fun place to be.

Several years ago I was trying to decide what my New Year's resolutions were going to be. I knew I could pick the standard ones of eating better, losing weight, and exercising more. While I knew those were important things to strive for, I really felt God asking me to consider what I wanted my walk with Him to look like that year. Would I be satisfied with the status quo, or would I be willing to walk on the journey He had set before me, wherever that might take me? Did I love Him enough to patiently wait for His direction and His timing or was I more bent on following my plans and ideas?

During that time, I had come across resolutions that Jonathan Edward had made and I decided to adopt his as my own for that year. They were simply this:

> Resolution One: I will live for God.
>
> Resolution Two: If no one else does, I still will.

Pretty basic, huh? Yes it was, but I really sensed it was what God was trying to get through to me. Following Him isn't rocket science; it's just living each and every day for Him, listening and obeying what He tells me to do. I realized that creating a masterpiece out of my life wasn't my responsibility–it was His. My responsibility was to be obedient during that year, and if I was, He would make something beautiful out of this "lump of clay" named LuAnn.

Believe it or not, I still have that sad-looking pinch pot that I made those many years ago. I decided to pull it out from the back of the closet and put it in my library as a reminder of my resolutions. I realized as I looked at it that on my own, my efforts don't amount to much, but with the Master Artist doing the work, I knew I could hold onto the words in 2 Corinthians 9:8, *"And God will generously provide all you need. Then you will always have everything you need and plenty left over to share with others."*

What a wonderful promise! I have found that this verse is true. God doesn't just provide; He provides generously and I love it that there is always plenty left over to share as I tell others about *my* Jesus!

My Jesus Prayer

> *Jesus, I am so thankful that You are the Master Artist of my life. All You ask of me is to be obedient and You will make something beautiful out of my life. Today I promise to live for You, even if no one else does.*

DAY 52

The Choice Is Yours to Make

For the grace of God has been revealed, bringing salvation to all people. And we are instructed to turn from godless living and sinful pleasures. We should live in this evil world with wisdom, righteousness, and devotion to God, while we look forward with hope to that wonderful day when the glory of our great God and Savior, Jesus Christ, will be revealed. He gave his life to free us from every kind of sin, to cleanse us, and to make us his very own people, totally committed to doing good deeds (Titus 2:11-14).

As I began to put a sermon together one day, I just couldn't shake a thought that kept going through my mind. Jesus rode into Jerusalem, hearing the shouts and praises from the crowds of people lining the streets. But just a few days later that same Jesus, tortured and beaten, walked to Golgotha, hearing the angry shouts to put Him to death. What happened? What went wrong? What changed the shouts of "Hosanna" to "Crucify Him"? I have bad weeks sometimes, but they don't hold a candle to Jesus' last week.

I guess what really blows my mind is the fact that as Jesus heard the "Hosannas," He already knew that the "Crucify Hims" were coming. It wasn't a surprise. It wasn't like He messed up and made the wrong choices throughout the week to cause the people to turn on Him. No, this was all part of His Father's plan, and even though Jesus prayed that the cup would be taken from Him, He knew that He would need to do whatever His Father asked. He knew He was sent to tell the people what they didn't want to hear and that it wouldn't win Him a popularity contest; but it wasn't about *His* fame, *His* comfort, or even *His* plan—it was about His Father's plan to sacrifice His Son for you and for me.

Am I willing to give that kind of sacrifice? Am I willing to do whatever my heavenly Father wants me to do, even when it isn't part of *my* plan? Even when it doesn't make me popular? Even when others may turn on me and hate me because of my willingness to stand for what is right? We are living in times when it isn't always easy to stand firm on biblical principles. We are being bombarded with the world shouting at us to lighten up and accept everyone's beliefs. They tell us that if it feels good—just do it. Unfortunately, if we give in to what the world is telling us to do we might as well be in the crowd shouting, "Crucify Him!"

As you go through your day, ask yourself what your behavior and your current choices are saying about your devotion to Christ and your sacrifice for Him. Are you shouting "Hosanna" or "Crucify Him"? No one can make the decision for you. The choice is yours.

My Jesus Prayer

Jesus, it's so easy for me to point my finger at those who cried, "Crucify Him," and neglect to stand up for You and Your Word. Forgive me, Father, and help me have the courage to make the right choices today.

DAY 53

The "Compare Game"

Purify me from my sins, and I will be clean; wash me, and I will be whiter than snow (Psalm 51:7).

I had a run-in with a knife, and I lost. I was working in my kitchen, and in a split second I found out that yes, my cutting utensil was sharp and it would do damage if it came in contact with my finger.

I knew by looking at the cut that it probably should have some stitches, but because "Go to doctor" was not on my list for the day (yes, in case you don't know, I am a compulsive list maker), I decided to just wrap it in gauze and keep completing my tasks. When my husband came home later, I showed it to him and said, "See, it doesn't look that bad." He gave me that *what am I going to do with you, LuAnn* look and said, "It doesn't look that good either."

What I learned through that episode in my life was that a relatively small cut can cause a lot of pain. I was reminded many times after that day that one of my fingers was injured, because it affected so many of my daily activities. I got very little sleep that night because of the throbbing, and because I work on a computer for a large portion of my day, typing was a real challenge. I was told once by one of my doctors that I am a "stout" woman, so you would think this small cut wouldn't have impacted a woman of my size and stature, but I can attest to the fact that it did.

My cut was a lot like sin. Many times we commit what we consider to be a relatively small sin, reasoning that it won't have any impact on our lives. We are so busy completing our "lists" that we don't think it is important to stop, repent, and be cleansed. It is so easy for us to compare our *small* sin to everyone else's *big* sin and feel justified in ignoring what we have done.

What we often fail to realize is that our *small* sin *does* affect us. We may not immediately feel the impact, but before long our ignored sins will begin to pile up and influence everything we do. We may look at ourselves and think that we really don't look that bad compared to everyone else, but the question is: Is God looking at us and saying we don't look that good? Playing the "compare game" can bring serious consequences.

Knowing the pain that my cut caused me, I've done all I can to never repeat my actions. My goal is to do the same thing with those sins that can easily creep into my life. Knowing the spiritual pain it can cause my Father *and* me, my plan is to do all I can to never repeat those sins again. Just like I couldn't ignore my physical pain, I want to be sensitive to the Lord's leading. I don't want to ignore those things that aren't pleasing to Him. I want my Savior to look at me and see His child who has been washed white as snow, not someone who has just covered up the mess.

How about you? Are there areas of your life that you know aren't pleasing to Him? Are you refusing to take the time to repent? Remember, no one else can repent for you; it is your responsibility to do that on your own. Don't delay. I'm confident the pain of admitting your transgression today won't be nearly as painful as it will be if you wait. He is waiting; why not talk with Him today?

My Jesus Prayer

Jesus, I know I need to spend time with You today, listening to Your every word. Show me where I have fallen short so that You can make me white as snow again.

DAY 54
Time To Be Fruitful

Remain in me, and I will remain in you. For a branch cannot produce fruit if it is severed from the vine, and you cannot be fruitful unless you remain in me (John 15:4).

I am highly allergic to certain fruits, namely peaches, oranges, and strawberries. Actually, I am not allergic to the fruit per se, but to the chemicals that are on them. Just walking through the produce section of a grocery store can often cause a reaction and touching a piece of these fruits can leave me quite ill.

It is because of this severe reaction that we garden and have our own fruit trees. As long as I know that the fruit has been grown organically, I am free to touch and eat these juicy delights. You can imagine then how thrilled I was one year to have our peach tree overloaded with fruit that I was able to eat, can, and freeze. Not only was I blessed with fruit from our tree, but my brother-in-law's tree was filled with more peaches than they could use, and a dear friend's trees were just calling us to go and pick from them, too. All in all, we processed around 200 pounds of peaches that we were able to enjoy all winter long!

When my brother-in-law told me that he had more fruit than they could use, I told him if there were others who wanted it, he could let them have it because our tree had produced so well. I'll be honest; his reply saddened me. He told me that he had offered the peaches to several people and they had shown interest in having the fruit. His only stipulation was that they would need to come to his home and help him pick the peaches. Without fail, every person replied, "Oh, if I have to pick them, then I don't want them." How sad. It wasn't a difficult job. I didn't even have to get on a ladder. I just stood under the tree and picked buckets full.

Unfortunately, this attitude is often seen among Christians concerning their walk and growth in the Lord. Oh, they want the benefits of being a Christian, but they don't want to have to put any time or effort in it. They are just happy to let their pastor do all the Bible reading and studying and then have him or her spoon-feed them on Sunday mornings. They want the blessings without the commitment. They want the rewards without the work.

I can't imagine how much this must sadden God. He loved us enough to send His one and only Son to die so we can spend eternity with Him, and we don't love Him enough to spend time daily, studying His Word, and communicating with Him through prayer. Our excuse? We're too busy. Really? Too busy to spend time with the Creator of the universe? Too busy to spend time with the One who loved us so much that He gave His all for us? Too busy to spend time with the King of Kings and Lord of Lords? I just can't imagine that any of us are *that* busy.

What may be even more disturbing is that we aren't grateful enough to tell others about His love for them and what He has done for them. People all around us are going to spend eternity in hell because we were too busy to let them know about our Jesus.

Our scripture today explains it so clearly. Those who need Christ will not be drawn to us if our lives are not filled with the fragrant fruit that only comes from being connected to the Vine.

Spending time with the Lord and allowing others to see His fruit in us is not a choice; it is a necessity. We are living in a world that is crying out for answers, and if we, as Christians, are not willing to make the effort to reach out to them, then we will have to answer for our actions. This is not the time to be selfish and lazy; it is the time to be fruitful.

My Jesus Prayer

> *Jesus, I know that it's easy for me to become so wrapped up in my agenda that I fail to spend time being connected to the Vine. Forgive me and help me to make our time together a priority so that others will see Your fruit in me.*

DAY 55
To Be or Not to Be…Selfish

Don't be selfish; don't try to impress others. Be humble, thinking of others as better than yourselves. Don't look out only for your own interests, but take an interest in others, too (Philippians 2:3-4).

Right on schedule, Valentine's Day arrived on February 14th. After taking a look on social media, it was obvious of the broad spectrum of peoples' feelings concerning that day. Plans ranged from couples not celebrating at all to ones who had scheduled an evening almost as spectacular as their wedding day. Just goes to show: different strokes for different folks.

We had just returned from a two-and-a-half-week vacation in Florida on February 13th, so we felt we had already done plenty of celebrating. Plus, I was to teach a class in the evening on Valentine's Day, so eating at home made the most sense. Dan offered to cook on the grill and I decided that the least I could do was make a special dessert for him. I knew that I had recently found an ooey-gooey chocolate dessert that sounded almost sinful and my taste buds began to water. I checked the ingredient list and was thrilled to see that I had everything necessary to make this wonderful delight (we live ten miles from town so running to the grocery store was not on my list).

Then it hit me. I had started this thought pattern with wanting to make a special dessert for Dan, but somewhere along the line I lost my focus and had ended up selecting a dessert that *I* would like. Dan likes chocolate, but if he is choosing a favorite confectionary, it always includes fruit, not chocolate. (I've tried to change him, but after all these years I think he is a lost cause.) So I put the sinful dessert recipe away and began my search for something *he* would like.

Why is it so easy for me to slip into my selfish desires? Not just with Dan, but with other relationships and, most importantly, my relationship with the Lord. If my desire is to look like Christ, then selfishness has no place in my choices or attitudes.

If you're unhappy today and feel unfulfilled, you may want to check your "selfish" quotient. Do your thoughts tend to turn toward yourself in most situations and do your decisions often benefit your own desires over others? If so, you may want to change the "recipe" for your life. Serving others and reaching out to make a difference in their life is sure to encourage your soul. If you aren't sure where to start, always begin by reading God's Word. The Bible has all the "ingredients" that you will need to live a fulfilled life that will show others your Jesus!

My Jesus Prayer

Jesus, I don't want to go through my life with a selfish attitude. Help me to be willing to sacrifice my wants and desires so that I can meet the needs of others. I know that only then will they see You in me.

DAY 56

The Test

I have hidden your word in my heart, that I might not sin against you. I praise you, O Lord; teach me your decrees. I have recited aloud all the regulations you have given us. I have rejoiced in your laws as much as in riches. I will study your commandments and reflect on your ways. I will delight in your decrees and not forget your word (Psalm 119:11-16).

We are going to pretend. Doesn't that make you feel like you're back in kindergarten? Let's pretend, heaven forbid, that we are all back in high school. On Monday morning our teacher hands us a new book and tells us that there will be a test on this book on Friday. We are to read the book during the week and be ready to take the test. Everything we need to know for the test is in the book, so it is important that we take the time to read all of it.

We take the book home and lay it on the table next to our bed. Every morning and every evening throughout the week we think about that book laying on the nightstand. We even hold the book on our head, hoping that will help the osmosis process of the words from the book getting into our brain. We never actually pick the book back up to read it, but figure that as long as we are lying next to the book each night, our brain waves will surely absorb what we need to know.

Friday arrives and we enter the class where the test will be taken. The teacher hands it out, and with our positive juices flowing, we feel confident that we will soar through the test with flying colors. But then we read the first question and realize that we have no clue what the main character's name was in the book. We try hard to remember even what the title of the book was, just in case that would give us an idea as to the person's name. We go on to question two, and then three, and then four, and by this time, beads of sweat are forming as we realize that we don't know the answers to any of them.

We approach the teacher's desk and explain to her that we are really upset and frustrated. We don't have a clue how we are supposed to answer these questions and nothing makes sense. We even explain to her that we are probably not going to be able to sleep tonight because we aren't going to pass this test. We do our best to convey how worried and stressed we are and that we are starting to feel sick. Surely she will understand our predicament and not make us finish the test.

But more than likely the teacher would look at us, and ask, "Did you read the book? All of the answers to the questions were in the book. Did you take time to read it?"

As we consider this scenario, we think to ourselves: *Well, duh, everyone knows that you can't learn from a book by osmosis.* We'd be fools to think otherwise and deserve to be frustrated and stressed if we didn't read the book that had the answers.

I'm guessing you know where I'm going with this today. We have God's Word available to us, which has everything we need to know in it, but how often do we actually pick it up and read it? Unfortunately, many people go through life stressed, frustrated, and feeling like they are at the end of their rope, wondering how in the world things will ever get better. All the while the answers are lying on their nightstand.

It would be a good idea if we all took time to evaluate how much time we are spending reading God's Word. Are we hiding His Word in our heart like our scripture today says? Are we rejoicing and delighting in His words?

Make it a priority today to spend time meditating on His Word. You just never know when life will throw you a test for which you will need the answers!

My Jesus Prayer

> *Jesus, I know that life will throw me tests, and I can either become stressed and frustrated, or I can meditate on Your Word for the answers. Help me to glean from Your wisdom each day, so that I will be ready for whatever comes my way.*

DAY 57

Transparency

I press on to reach the end of the race and receive the heavenly prize for which God, through Christ Jesus, is calling us (Philippians 3:14).

When I began writing, the Lord impressed on me that I needed to be transparent with my readers. I needed to let them know that I'm just like them, trying my best to walk each day with the Lord, but often falling short and needing His grace. Well, I feel led to be transparent with you again today, so if you have had your fill of my life, you may want to skip today's devotional!

Our area was in an extreme drought. If I would have had a dollar for every time I had prayed for rain that summer, I would have been fairly wealthy. We desperately needed it at our house. We had watched the radar many times when it showed that rain was heading straight for us, but inevitably it would split, and some would go to the north and the rest to the south, leaving us high and dry. At one point, a town thirty-five miles from us received four inches in a week and we got less than a half of an inch.

What a surprise it was when I woke up one Sunday morning and heard not just rain, but heavy rain. It was pouring! I jumped out of bed, got on my knees, and praised the Lord for answering my prayers. Well, I guess I really didn't jump out of bed and, if I'm honest, I didn't get on my knees either. Even more embarrassing to admit, I didn't even give praise to the Lord. Believe it or not, and trust me when I say I'm not proud of this: Instead of praising, I whined.

I think my whining went something like this, "Lord, are you kidding me? Rain on Sunday morning? You know how easily our electricity goes out. What if we lose power before I can get a shower? My hair is sticking out more than a porcupine's quills, so I won't be going anywhere if I can't do something with it. You are just going to have to keep the power on, Lord, if you want me to go to church to praise and worship You!"

Pretty sad, huh? I had prayed and prayed, and begged and begged, and pleaded and pleaded for rain, and then when my prayer was answered, I complained. Not much of an example, and definitely not someone who desires to look like her Jesus. The problem was that instead of keeping my focus upward, my focus was inward.

Now I'm sure you are waiting with baited breath to find out what happened. You will be relieved to know that our power stayed on that day and I was able to get the quills under control. We even made it to church to give praise to the One I should have been praising earlier. And yes, in the meantime, I came to my senses and asked the Lord to forgive me for my selfishness and thanked Him for the much-needed rain.

I'm sharing this with you for two reasons. First, to remind you that walking with Christ is a journey. It's a journey that won't be perfect and won't end until we meet Him face-to-face. On our voyage with Him we will, at times, lose our focus and react differently than we should. It's at those times that we need to acknowledge our sin, ask for forgiveness, and move on. Too often we dwell on our past sins, bringing them up over and over again, which in turn takes our focus off of Him and onto us again. It's a vicious cycle that we can easily fall into, and we need to remember that Satan wants nothing better than to keep us in turmoil. We do not serve a God of turmoil. We serve a God of forgiveness and peace and we are supposed to press on to reach the end of our race.

Secondly, I'm sharing this as a reminder that others need to see us being transparent. Too many times we try to act differently than we really are. We can come across to the world that because we are Christians, we are better than everyone else and that we are perfect. We will never reach the lost with that kind of attitude. Remember, God doesn't "rank" sins. My sin of selfishness was no less a sin than that of a liar, thief, or murderer. We need to let others know that we are all sinners, but through Christ we are saved by His grace, and they can be, too.

I'm so thankful that Christ's love for me *never* changes, even when I don't behave like I should. It is because of that love, because of the amazing sacrifice that He made for me, that I want to serve Him. So I'm going to keep truckin,' keep pedaling, keep putting one foot in front of another, holding His hand, and trusting that His ways and timing are perfect, even when it rains on a Sunday morning!

My Jesus Prayer

Jesus, I am far from perfect and I often mess up by focusing inward instead of upward. Thank You for loving me even when I fail You, and for Your willingness to hold my hand as You lead me back on the right path.

LUANN GERIG FULTON

DAY 58

The Swing Set

Give your burdens to the Lord, and he will take care of you. He will not permit the godly to slip and fall (Psalm 55:22).

When our children were small we purchased a swing set for our backyard. It wasn't one of the huge jungle gyms like you often see in backyards today. It was just a simple design with a few swings and a glider. It wasn't fancy, but it gave our kids many hours of enjoyment.

It seems as though we blinked and our children were all grown and the swing set sat empty. As each year passed, it looked a little worse for wear and slowly became an eyesore. Several different times my husband wanted to get rid of it, but I always put a stop to the idea. I knew it needed to go but I didn't want to accept the fact that it was past its prime. Somehow I had become comfortable with how it looked, even though it was rusty and broken down.

Because of its location, the swing set had to be moved each time I mowed, and lifting it caused me to have back pain. But even that didn't deter me from wanting to hold onto this piece of equipment. The last straw was when I used the excuse that we would need it someday when we had grandchildren and Dan looked at me and said, "Do you really think you would put your grandchildren on those swings?" That question was finally what I needed to hear to realize action had to be taken, because I knew I would never put any child on something that wasn't safe.

This will probably sound strange, but the day that Dan hauled away our swing set, I felt as though something had been lifted from me. At that moment I realized how tightly I had been holding onto something that needed to be released. What started out to be a good thing had eventually been affecting me in a negative way.

I've been thinking lately about the fact that this is sometimes how sin enters our lives. Sin doesn't always begin by being a sin. That new friendship that you have developed at your workplace with a member of the opposite sex might have begun in a very innocent way, but as time has gone by, it has slowly become more than just a friendship. You know it's wrong and you need to put a stop to it and confess your sin, but you have become comfortable with the ugliness of the situation and rationalized its existence.

Maybe using food, alcohol, or drugs to lower your stress level is your sin. You have forgotten (or refused to admit) that your body is the temple of God, and putting anything into it that isn't pleasing to Him is not bringing Him honor or glory. Maybe you are rationalizing that overeating is something that only affects you so it is okay, but deep down we know that that argument doesn't hold water either.

Spend some time evaluating every area of your life and see if there is anything that you are holding onto that needs to be released. If you discover something that is causing you to sin, confess it to God and then loosen your white-knuckle grip on it. If you do this, I believe you will have that same "burden-lifted feeling" come over you. It will give you a fresh start and oh, what a good feeling that will be!

My Jesus Prayer

Jesus, show me if my hands are holding onto things that should be given to You. I know that You alone can take my burdens and sin away, but I have to be willing to give them up first.

DAY 59

Wandering Minds

No one can serve two masters. For you will hate one and love the other; you will be devoted to one and despise the other. You cannot serve God and be enslaved to money (Matthew 6:24).

Do you have problems with your mind wandering? I sure do. There are times when I sit down to write and the next thing I know I'm thinking about what I need to put on my grocery list, what I'm fixing for dinner, or better yet, what restaurant my husband should take me to next! My mind doesn't wander because I don't like writing, because I do. It's just that I have a lot going on in my life and it's often hard to focus on just one thing.

I was reading recently and came across this statement, "Whatever occupies your mind the most becomes your god." I shared a similar statement with you before and it was convicting to me then, just as this one was now. Both times it made me give some thought to what brainwaves occupy my mind the most. Are my thoughts wholesome? Are they selfish? Are they vindictive? Are they spiritually based or worldly based?

The key words in this statement are "the most." In other words, all of us have times when our minds wander and we have trouble focusing, but this is asking us to contemplate what thoughts occupy our mind *the most*. They may not be bad thoughts, but whatever they are shows us what our main focus is and what our "god" is. Thinking about our favorite hobby or sport is okay, but if that's what we think about the most, then it is our god. Thinking about making more money is not a bad thing, but if the majority of our thoughts are consumed with getting rich, money has become our god. Exercising is a good thing, but, believe it or not, I've actually known people who are obsessed with it, and as a result their own bodies become their god.

We read in Exodus 20:3, *"You must not have any other god but me."* Scripture makes it very clear that we are to only worship the one true God. He refuses to take second place in our lives, but as I mentioned before, it is our choice. We can choose what or who our god is by the decisions we make and by the thoughts that we allow to permeate our minds. It is our choice if we allow our worries, fears, and doubts to control us and become our god. As a result, because we cannot serve two masters, we send the message to *the* God that He is a liar and cannot be trusted.

As you go through your day, take note of which thoughts are occupying your mind *the most*. You may even want to write them down so at the end of the day you can have a clearer picture of what or who your god is. If it isn't the one true God, then you need to change your priorities and ask the Holy Spirit to control your thoughts. He is willing, able, and waiting for your decision.

My Jesus Prayer

> *Jesus, my thoughts often wander and I can easily lose my focus. Help me to steer my thoughts towards You and what You would have me do today. May I worship You and You alone as I go throughout my day.*

DAY 60
Save a Seat For Me

There is more than enough room in my Father's home. If this were not so, would I have told you that I am going to prepare a place for you? When everything is ready, I will come and get you, so that you will always be with me where I am. And you know the way to where I am going (John 14:2-4).

The scene played out as if it was in a movie. The older couple returned to the waiting room after seeing the doctor and moved toward two empty chairs. As the woman walked closer, it sounded as if she was attempting to muffle the sounds that were coming from her mouth. She dropped her weary body into the chair next to her husband and spoke the words, "I've just been given a death sentence," as sobs overtook her small frame.

The husband wrapped his arm around her and waited for her to speak again. She looked into his eyes and whispered, "I thought there was hope, but that isn't what the doctor just said. You heard him. He said if I take treatments I will probably be sick every day I have left and regardless, I don't have much time left." At that point the cries could not be stifled as her husband gently kissed her forehead.

It was obvious that this man, who had more than likely been by her side for many years, was at a loss for words. He finally said, "Well, we both knew we wouldn't live forever, and this may mean that you get to go to heaven before me. But if you do, don't forget to save a seat for me."

I wish this had been a scene from a movie; instead it was a real-life moment that I witnessed in the cancer center one day as I sat with my mother-in-law awaiting her treatment. I sat there fighting tears myself as I watched the reality of life and death play out in front of me. I didn't know this couple, but hearing their dialogue had suddenly allowed me a glimpse into what life had dealt them and, more than likely, the dark days ahead.

I have replayed this scene over and over in my mind since then. The thing that I keep thinking is that more than likely, this woman's first thought when she received this diagnosis wasn't: *Well, I wish I had made more money in my life. Or, if I had just climbed higher on the corporate ladder, this moment would be easier. Or, if I would have just had a nicer home than my neighbors, then I would have been ready for my life to come to an end.*

None of that mattered—not at this moment. I'm guessing that she would have traded anything that she possessed to receive a more positive diagnosis. But the fact was that nothing she possessed on this earth could make her doctor's words less painful.

I think it is often easier for us to see this kind of reality when we are looking into someone else's life. It makes sense that "things" don't really mean anything at the end of life when we are critiquing another soul. But when it is us, it's different. We spend our time trying to possess more and more beautiful things, ascending one more rung on the corporate ladder, driving that nicer car, or owning a more prestigious home. In our pursuit, we can easily rationalize. We believe we deserve it because we worked hard and we are entitled to have it all. Unfortunately, we too will someday face the reality that none of this mattered, that we won't enter heaven's gates because of what we owned, but because of who we knew.

All of us know that we won't live forever and none of us know when we will face eternity. As a result, it is vital that we spend our days doing things that will affect eternity, not our pocketbooks. Christ won't ask for our bank statement or our tax records. He won't ask us if our parents or spouse were Christians, because they won't be able to get us into heaven. He will only be concerned with whether or not He has been our focus. He gave His life so we can spend eternity with Him and He has a seat reserved for each of us. The question is, when He calls for us, will we be ready?

My Jesus Prayer

Jesus, I know that it is my decision alone as to whether I will spend eternity with You. No one else can get me in; it is up to me to accept You as my Lord and Savior. In You alone will I put my trust.

LUANN GERIG FULTON

DAY 61

The Oven

This means that anyone who belongs to Christ has become a new person. The old life is gone; a new life has begun! (2 Corinthians 5:17).

I will be the first to admit that I love modern conveniences. I have no interest in going camping on my vacations because I would have to leave those wonderful appliances at home. When we get done eating a meal, I am thankful to have a dishwasher that does a big share of the cleanup. It makes me happy that I have a refrigerator that keeps my food cold and a freezer that keeps my food frozen. When our clothes get dirty, I don't have to go out and find a rock to beat them on. I just put them in my washer that cleans them for me and then my drier that dries them to my liking. Some people would call me spoiled, and I would probably have to agree.

One of my favorite modern conveniences is my self-cleaning oven. I realized one day that a couple things had boiled over in it, making it look rather nasty. Being the "odd" person that I am, looking at my oven in that condition made me a little nervous. It made me think about the fact that if I was unexpectedly hospitalized or suddenly died and someone else came into my home, they would see that grime in my oven. I would be mortified. (I have the same feeling when I find penicillin growing in my refrigerator, and yes, the men in white coats are probably on their way to get me right now.)

To remedy this "crisis," I walked over to the oven, pushed a button and the cleaning process began. In just a few hours, the grease and grime were gone and I could relax with the knowledge that if the Lord called me home, I wouldn't be embarrassed about my oven's interior.

As I checked out my newly cleaned oven, I had this thought: I sure wish it were this easy to remove those things in my life that aren't very pretty. I wish I could just push a button and someone else would wash all my impurities away – my sometimes critical spirit, my lack of patience, my lack of faith and trust in my Lord.

Then it hit me. I *do* have Someone more than capable of removing these things from my life! Jesus is just waiting for me to confess the grungy grime that often starts with just a small stain and then builds and builds when I allow it. The amazing thing is that once I go to the master "cleaner," He immediately scrubs every last speck of dirt away and washes me white as snow. It doesn't even take a few hours; it is instantaneous.

Is there something in your past or in your present that you don't think the Lord can forgive? If so, you are wrong. Maybe you are worried that your time on earth may suddenly end and it won't be the dirt in your oven that will embarrass you, but the sin in your life. I want you to know that it doesn't matter what the sin is – whether it's a new stain or something that has been building up for years and years—He is able to make you a new creation immediately. And I guarantee that at that moment, you will feel renewed and refreshed as you revel in the fact that you are a forgiven child of the King!

My Jesus Prayer

> *Jesus, it is easy to dwell on my past transgressions, thinking that they are unforgiveable. Help me to remember that You are capable of removing those things in an instant. All I need to do is ask.*

DAY 62

Let's Do This!

Now all glory to God, who is able, through his mighty power at work within us, to accomplish infinitely more than we might ask or think. Glory to him in the church and in Christ Jesus through all generations forever and ever! Amen (Ephesians 3:20-21).

There are times in my life when I feel like I am floundering. Maybe you know that feeling. It's those times when we just aren't sure what Jesus is trying to tell us and our future seems obscure. I really don't like those times in my life, but if I take a look at my past, I can see where Jesus has always come through in His timing. I remember once when I began to sense that He wanted me to stop dwelling on what I *couldn't* do and start focusing on what He *could* do through me. I needed to allow Him to use the difficulties that I was facing for His glory and not use them as excuses. I had to be willing to live beyond the limits of my comfort zone so that the Lord could accomplish great things through me for His glory.

But I knew that there was a huge problem when attempting this: Satan doesn't like this at all. He didn't want me to accomplish anything for Jesus, especially if it drew others to want Him as their Lord and Savior. Satan wanted me to remain stagnant, living inside my protective bubble and settling for the status quo. Unfortunately, it's really easy for me to want to remain there too.

I have written before that I have a lot of respect for Corrie ten Boom and the amazing testimony she had throughout her life, even when she was in the worst of circumstances. When she spoke, her words were powerful and they are still having a huge impact on others long after she received her eternal reward. Corrie was a child of God who wasn't afraid of pushing herself way beyond her human capabilities, knowing that wherever God led her, He would give her exactly what she needed every step of the way.

I read a quote of hers one day that was exactly what I needed. Her timely words were, "When we are powerless to do a thing, it is a great joy that we can come and step inside the ability of Jesus." In other words, when Satan is whispering over and over in my ear that I can't do something, that I am too weak to accomplish a task, I can smile right back at him and yell, "You are right, Satan! I can't, but *He* can!"

What a difference it makes when we realize whose abilities and power we can tap into! There isn't anything that we will face that is beyond Christ's capabilities. There isn't any detour on our journey that He doesn't know about, and He is fully aware of where we will end up. Nothing surprises Him. Nothing makes Him fret and nothing overwhelms Him. We can be assured that no matter what, His answer to us is, "Don't worry, I've got this!"

Are you living in fear of what you might face tomorrow? Are you afraid that if you commit to live completely sold out to Christ, He will ask you to do things that are way beyond your ability? You are right; He probably will! He already knows that you can't do it by yourself, but with His help you can! All He needs is your willingness to let Him lead and He will take care of the rest.

I'm guessing there will be times when you and I feel powerless in the days ahead. Let's not forget that we have the privilege of "stepping inside the ability of Jesus." Just the thought of that gives me chills. Let's do this!

My Jesus Prayer

> *Jesus, help me to remember that when I think I'm not strong enough, You are! Thank You so much for allowing me to step inside Your abilities and receive the power that is needed for today.*

LUANN GERIG FULTON

DAY 63
What Will I Leave Behind?

Dear brothers and sisters, pattern your lives after mine, and learn from those who follow our example (Philippians 3:17).

It was a week filled with sorrow. First we attended the funeral of a relative who had passed away from liver cancer. The next day, our beloved aunt walked through the gates of heaven after her valiant fight with the same cancer. Then just two days later, a very dear friend of ours met his Jesus face-to-face following his diagnosis of brain and lung cancer. All three of them were dearly loved by their friends and family and will be greatly missed.

I cannot attend a funeral or hear of someone passing away without thinking of my own mother who left this earth in 2009. She was especially on my mind that week because she was celebrating another birthday in heaven. Oh, how I wish we could have celebrated together on her special day, but I have a feeling that the party in heaven was much more than I could ever imagine!

For those who leave this earth after accepting Jesus Christ as their personal Lord and Savior, eternity is spent walking streets of gold and worshiping the King of Kings. They are completely healed with no more pain, no more cancer, and no more heartache. They close their eyes to the problems of this world and open them in their new heavenly home.

It is us who are left behind who grieve, who now have to deal with facing each day with an empty hole that no one else can fill. Life will never be the same for us who are left behind. We must carry on without those whom we dearly loved.

After my mom passed away, I knew I had a choice to make. I could dwell on the fact that she left me, or I could dwell on *what* she left me. She left me to receive her eternal reward, but what she left *for* me was an example of how a Christian life should look. She left me with memories of the times when I saw her respond in a loving way when I wasn't very lovable. She left me with memories of seeing her spend time in the Word, learning more and more from her Jesus. She left me with memories of always displaying the image of her heavenly Father, so much that I never heard anyone say a negative word about her.

What she left me were very big shoes to fill in her absence. She left me with an example of what I should strive for in my walk with my heavenly Father each and every day. I often think of her and wonder what she would do in certain situations and wish I could glean from her wisdom just one more time. But because I know that her wisdom came from spending time with her Jesus, I know that I have the same opportunity each day to learn from Him, too.

A friend asked me once if I spent much time at my mother's grave and I admitted that I have only been there twice since 2009. That may shock you and you may feel like I'm not a very good daughter, but my reason is that she is not there. I have no "pull" to her gravesite because she taught me by her example, that in death, she would have eternal life with the Lord. Her steadfast focus was on the day she would step on heaven's shore and touch the hand of the One she served so faithfully.

When the Lord calls me home, I wonder what I will leave behind for those I love here on earth. Will I be remembered for telling others about my Jesus or for living only for my own pleasure? Will others remember me as being a faithful follower of His or a faithful follower of the world? I know that the example that I leave behind could either draw others closer to my Savior or push them farther away. I need to be diligent in making the right choices now, so what I leave behind will make a difference in eternity. Time is short and I need to be faithful today.

How about you? When God calls you home, will your passing just be a date in an obituary, or will your life live on by what you have left behind? Time is short. You need to be faithful today.

My **Jesus Prayer**

> *Jesus, I am blessed to have ancestors who set an example for me as to how I should live for You, but I know that they will not get me into heaven. It is my decision whether I will be an example for those who will come after me. Help me serve You in such a way that will help others serve You, too.*

DAY 64

Memories

Every time I think of you, I give thanks to my God (Philippians 1:3).

Dan and I hit the road one day to visit my sister and her husband in Atlanta. They had recently moved there and this was the first time we would see their new surroundings.

What a great time we had catching up on each other's lives. During our last evening together, my brother-in-law asked each of us to recall our earliest childhood memory. What followed was lots of laughter while we reminisced about the days gone by.

Memories. All of us have them. Some are good and bring smiles to our faces and warmth to our hearts. Some are not so good, but we can see how we grew from the negative experiences. Unfortunately, some are so painful that we have pushed them back into the deepest recesses of our mind and they have taken deep root in how we live each day.

The hardest thing to grasp sometimes is that there is nothing we can do to change any of our memories. We can't get a redo on anything that has transpired in our lives whether it was good, bad, or ugly. Unfortunately, I think we spend much of our time trying to do just that. We either try to relive the good times instead of making today better, or we rehash the negative memories over and over again until they consume our every thought.

I think it is important for each of us to remember that we may never know how important a moment is until we look back on it. What is happening today, at this very moment, might either be a memory that you will want to forget or one that you want to cherish. We have the opportunity to make memories today, tomorrow, and in the weeks and months to come that make a difference in our life and in the lives of others, either positively or negatively.

Memories. What kind are you and I leaving behind today? Just as we talked about yesterday, all of us have a choice to make. I love what Paul wrote in our scripture for today. How wonderful it would be if this could be written about each of us, and what a wonderful goal for which we should strive. Whether this happens will be determined by the choices we make and in whom we have our faith and focus. If we are intentional in making sure that what we do today is in line with Jesus' will, I have a feeling that the memories we make will be much brighter, and those that we leave for others to reflect on will bring a smile to their faces and warmth to their hearts. Let's do everything we can so those we meet will want to thank God for allowing us to be a part of their lives.

My Jesus Prayer

Jesus, I want to make memories today that will have a positive impact on eternity. May those who come behind me be thankful for the life I lived and deem me an example that they want to follow.

ASK ME ABOUT MY JESUS

DAY 65
Lord, Help Me

For I am not ashamed of this Good News about Christ. It is the power of God at work, saving everyone who believes – the Jew first and also the Gentile (Romans 1:16).

Florida is a great place to visit in the winter. As I have written before, I am not a fan of cold weather, so we usually try to escape for a few days to a warmer climate sometime during the winter each year.

Whenever we travel, we try hard to not eat in too many chain restaurants. I usually spend time scouring the Internet for eating establishments in the area to which we are traveling. We love to try out the locally owned "Mom and Pop" style restaurants where most of the locals eat. We have been doing this for quite a few years and I don't believe we were ever steered wrong, and as a result have found some amazing, out of the way eateries which we return to when we are in the area.

Of all the local places we have experienced, there is one that probably stands above all the others in my opinion. We found it some years ago when we were in the Orlando area, and anyone who knows me well will not be shocked to find out that it was an ice cream shop.

I am rather strange in the fact that I rarely eat any ice cream at home. I seldom buy it at the grocery store and when I do, it usually gets nasty before it is consumed. But that changes when I find a really good place of business that specializes in this particular dessert. That's when my willpower often goes out the window and I thoroughly enjoy every single bite.

While perusing the Internet, I came across raving reviews about this ice cream shop. Person after person said it was by far the best ice cream they had ever eaten. These people hadn't just heard about it, they had experienced it firsthand, so they had the authority to let others know their opinions.

What makes their ice cream so much better is the fact that it is made right in front of you. You decide what you want in your personal concoction and then, using liquid nitrogen, your ice cream is made from milk right before your eyes. The result? The creamiest, most amazing frozen delight you will ever experience. They say that they have the most amazing ice cream under the sun, and I have to agree.

I can't tell you how many people we have told about this establishment. We have shown others pictures of our visits there and tried to describe just how incredible their ice cream is in our opinion. It isn't just a place we have heard about or read about; it is a place we have experienced for ourselves and ice cream that we have indulged in several different times. We tell others because we want them to try it too, because we believe they will like it just as much as we do. Why would we want to keep quiet about something that we think is so incredible?

I have realized that this is how we should be about telling others about our Jesus. Talk about someone incredible! He came to the earth to experience everything we will ever face and then endured an agonizing death on a cross for our sins. Then He rose again so that we could live forever with Him in eternity. Now *that* is something to talk about. It's not just something we have heard about, because those of us who have accepted Him into our hearts as our Lord and Savior have experienced Him. We know firsthand what an awesome God we serve and we should be sharing our knowledge with everyone with whom we come in contact.

But for some reason, it's often much easier to talk about ice cream. Bragging on a frozen dessert doesn't step on anyone's toes, doesn't make us feel uncomfortable, and doesn't push us out of our comfort zones. And more than likely, sharing about ice cream won't cause anyone to reject us either. It's just so much safer, isn't it? Even though experiencing good food satisfies us for just a fleeting moment and experiencing a relationship with Christ is for eternity, we still often choose comfort over someone's eternal destination.

> *Lord, forgive me.*
>
> *Lord, forgive me for my laziness, selfishness, and lack of concern for the salvation of others.*
>
> *Lord, help me to realize how short time is and the urgency with which I should be sharing about my Jesus.*

Why in the world would I want to keep quiet about my Jesus who I know to be so incredible?

My Jesus Prayer

> *Jesus, help me to not be ashamed of the gospel. Help me to be more excited to tell others about You than anything else in my life. May my life show others just how incredible You are!*

DAY 66

Not Once!

So God created human beings in his own image. In the image of God he created them; male and female he created them (Genesis 1:27).

I was thinking one day about all the times in my life that I have looked in the mirror and didn't like what I saw. The times that I have wished I was like someone else.

Why can't I be as pretty as she is?

Why can't I be as thin as she is?

Why can't I be as creative as he or she is?

Why wasn't I given the athletic ability with which he or she was blessed?

Why can't I be as smart as he or she is?

Why can't I write as well as he or she can?

I could go on and on with my list. There have been many times when what I saw in the mirror just didn't measure up to my perspective of "perfection."

But if I believe what the Bible says in Genesis, then I also have to believe that not once has God looked at me and thought:

I sure wish LuAnn was as pretty as _____.

I sure wish LuAnn was as thin as _____.

I sure wish LuAnn had the same creative ability as _____.

I sure wish LuAnn was as athletic as _____.

I sure wish LuAnn was as smart as _____.

I sure wish LuAnn could write as well as _____.

Not once has He done this. God created me to be me, and if I waste a lot of time in my life trying to be someone else, I will miss out on who and what I really am. I am a child of God that was created in *His* image. I am a child of God who is so dearly loved that He sent His one and only Son, Jesus, to die on a cross for my sins. I am a child of God that has accepted Him as my Lord and Savior, and as a result I have a home that is being prepared for me in heaven where I will spend eternity with my Jesus.

The exciting news? The same is true for you! Not once has He looked at you and wished you were more like _____(insert the name of your choice). Not once has God looked at you and thought He had made a huge mistake. Not once! You were also created in His image and He loves you more than you can ever imagine. And He loves you just the way you are right now.

Yes, He loves you and me with all of our flaws and imperfections, and nothing we have done and no imperfection we might have can diminish His love for us. I don't know about you, but that just blows my mind.

Does that mean that we should never strive to change those qualities that hinder us from looking like Jesus? Of course not. Striving to reflect His image should be our focus every day. We should always make choices that we know will please Him. It is a continuous process in which He loves us where we are today, but wants even greater things for us tomorrow. Why? Because He loves us that much.

So today when you look in the mirror, don't concentrate on what or who you aren't. Concentrate on who created you and in whose image you were created. Remember, God never makes a mistake, so He didn't make a mistake when He made you, and He loves you right where you are today!

My Jesus Prayer

Jesus, I wonder if I hurt You when I look in the mirror and wish I were someone else. Help me to remember that You created me and know everything about me. May I be all that You desire for me to be as I strive to be a fully devoted follower of You.

LUANN GERIG FULTON

DAY 67

Because I Said So

For the word of the Lord holds true, and we can trust everything he does (Psalm 33:4).

There are certain Bible stories which most people probably know: Adam and Eve, Noah building the ark, and David and Goliath are just a few of them. I came across another story one day in my devotional reading that I have read and heard many times. But something jumped out at me on this particular morning as I read about Jesus raising Lazarus from the dead, something I had never noticed before.

Most of us are familiar with the main points of this event: Lazarus lived in Bethany with his sisters, Mary and Martha, and they were very close friends with Jesus. In this story, Lazarus became very ill, so his sisters quickly sent a message to Jesus, telling Him of the state of their brother. I'm guessing that they thought that Jesus would immediately drop whatever He was doing to come to Lazarus's bedside and heal him. But that wasn't what happened. When He received the news, Jesus said, *"Lazarus's sickness will not end in death. No, it happened for the glory of God so that the Son of God will receive glory from this* (John 11:4)." Then, instead of rushing to heal him, Jesus stayed right where He was for two more days.

By the time Jesus did arrive in Bethany, He was informed that Lazarus had died and had been in the grave for four days. As you can imagine, Mary and Martha were distraught at the death of their brother and told Jesus that if He would have only come right away, He could have healed him. In verse 23 of John 11, we read that Jesus told Martha that her brother would rise again, but when Jesus told Martha this she thought He was talking about the last day when all Christians will rise.

As Jesus saw how distraught Mary and Martha were, along with many of their friends, He became angry at their unbelief of what He could do. We read in John 11:33-44, *"When Jesus saw her weeping and saw the other people wailing with her, a deep anger welled up within him, and he was deeply troubled. 'Where have you put him?' he asked them. They told him, 'Lord, come and see.' Then Jesus wept. The people who were standing nearby said, 'See how much he loved him!' But some said, 'This man healed a blind man. Couldn't he have kept Lazarus from dying?' Jesus was still angry as he arrived at the tomb, a cave with a stone rolled across its entrance. 'Roll the stone aside,' Jesus told them. But Martha, the dead man's sister, protested, 'Lord, he has been dead for four days. The smell will be terrible.' Jesus responded, 'Didn't I tell you that you would see God's glory if you believe?' So they rolled the stone aside. Then Jesus looked up to heaven and said, 'Father, thank you for hearing me. You always hear me, but I said it out loud for the sake of all these people standing here, so that they will believe you sent me.' Then Jesus shouted, 'Lazarus, come out!' And the dead man came out, his hands and feet bound in graveclothes, his face wrapped in a headcloth. Jesus told them, 'Unwrap him and let him go!'"* Can you imagine how everyone's jaws dropped as Lazarus made his appearance!

I have read this story many times, but what hit me on this particular day was the fact that Jesus told them to roll the stone away. Why did He tell them to do this? If He could raise Lazarus from the dead by just speaking a word, surely He could have just told the stone to move and it would have done so, without the help of those in attendance.

Could it be that Jesus wanted them to trust Him enough to perform the simple act of rolling the stone to the side? Martha was hesitant to have this done because she knew the odor would be overwhelming, but Jesus wanted her to trust Him enough to do as she was told. I think if I would have been Jesus, I would have said something to the effect of, "Are you kidding me, Martha? How many times have I proved My power to you? When will you understand that I can do far more than you can ever imagine, if you would just believe in Me and do what I tell you to do?"

Jesus needed Martha, Mary, and everyone else there to believe in Him enough to go ahead and roll that stone away. I have to admit that as I thought about this, my first response was also one of unbelief that they didn't trust Him enough to obey Him. Then it hit me between the eyes. How many times in my life has Jesus asked me to do something and I have balked? I've questioned His motives. I've reminded Him of all the bad things that can happen if I did what He was asking of me. I've dragged my feet, hoping He would change His mind and let me go another route: all because I didn't trust.

There were times when I was raising our children that they questioned me as to why they had to do a particular task. Oftentimes, my response was, "Because I said so." I expected them to obey just because I spoke the words. I have a feeling that it is no different with my heavenly Father. I'm guessing that those times I have kept whining and asking why, He just wanted to say to me, "Because I said so."

How about you? Is Jesus asking you to do something, but instead of believing and trusting in His power, you just keep asking "Why?" I imagine if you take the time today to be still and listen for His voice, you just might hear Him say, "Because I said so."

My Jesus Prayer

Jesus, thank You for your patience with me as I learn to trust You. Help me to have the courage to immediately say yes to whatever You ask me to do, even if it doesn't make sense to me.

DAY 68
Imposing Our Way

So why do you condemn another believer? Why do you look down on another believer? Remember, we will all stand before the judgment seat of God. For the Scriptures say, "As surely as I live," says the Lord, "every knee will bend to me, and every tongue will declare allegiance to God." Yes, each of us will give a personal account to God. So let's stop condemning each other. Decide instead to live in such a way that you will not cause another believer to stumble and fall (Romans 14:10-13).

It was just a few short weeks before we would be welcoming another grandson into our family. It was so exciting when the time remaining was finally just weeks, instead of months!

Things would change in our daughter's home. Their oldest son, Elias, who was twenty-two months at the time, would no longer be the center of attention. He'd now have to share the limelight with this brand-new wiggly, sometimes crying, precious little one. Up until then, he had only known this baby as being in his mommy's tummy. Now he would have to adjust to his brother being around, sometimes noisy and even annoying.

Of course, things would change for Elias's parents too. While they already knew that taking care of a young one who was nearly two was exhausting, they would now discover a new level of fatigue. They would now add a baby who would be entirely dependent on them. They'd be up throughout the night, and lack of sleep would most likely become their norm for a time. Not only would they be helping their new little one adjust to living in his new surroundings, they would have a two-year-old asking questions at every turn.

The word I thought of when I contemplated what they would all face is *change*. Lots of changes were on their horizon, and there was no way they could know or even understand those changes until they were in the middle of them. Those who had already experienced it could have told them all about it over and over again, but until they experienced it for themselves it was almost impossible for them to understand. They could read every book ever written about how to handle multiple children, but until they actually had two children in their home, they couldn't truly know what it would be like.

No two children are alike. What happened with someone else's children may never happen to theirs. More than likely, they would discover that what works in someone else's home in juggling their new schedule, may not work at all in their home. They would have to experience it themselves and figure out what is the best for their own family. Instead of trying to measure up to what others told them was the right way, they would just need to keep their focus on Christ each and every day and allow Him to lead them as they raised their family for Him.

The same is true in our Christian family. No two of us are the same, and what happens in my life may not ever happen in yours. What works for me in my walk with Christ may not work at all in yours. Likewise (and this may make us squirm), what Christ convicts me of that needs changing in my life may not be what He convicts you about, and vice versa. Each of us is at a different stage in our Christian walk, and as a result He will do exactly what we need at the time that is perfect for us individually, so His direction for each of us is not the same.

Unless we have walked in the shoes of others, there is a good chance that we can't understand exactly what they are going through. We can sympathize, console and pray for them, and even share with them what has helped us. But at some point, they will need to face their own changes and learn to rely on Christ's leading for their particular situation.

I wonder how many people we have hurt or scared away from walking with Christ because we imposed our way of doing things on them. Instead of humbly pointing them toward Christ and loving them through their journey, we've demanded that they do it our way, when our way may not have been what was best for them. Unfortunately, our way isn't always Christ's way and imposing our thoughts on others can often do more harm than good. It is important that anything we share is based on biblical principles as we come alongside those who need to know that we care. Others will be helped much more if they can see Christ in us on a daily basis. How we act and respond to others will speak much louder than what actually comes out of our mouths.

Just as it is not my responsibility to demand that my daughter's family do things exactly like I would, it is not my responsibility to do the convicting in other people's lives. Again, I can share biblical principles, sympathize, console, and pray with those I know, but it is Christ's responsibility to do the convicting. My job is to be willing to walk with those who are hurting, loving them where they are today, and making sure it is evident that Christ lives in me. I am confident that if we do this as we focus on pointing others toward Christ, our actions will speak much louder than our words.

My Jesus Prayer

*Jesus, help me to want to share my story with others,
but not demand that they always do as I have done.
Keep me mindful that each of us are unique, and that
You will mold us according to Your perfect plan.*

LUANN GERIG FULTON

DAY 69

At His Feet

Her sister, Mary, sat at the Lord's feet, listening to what he taught (Luke 10:39).

Mary and Martha. What a pair they were. Martha was always running around, making sure everything was just perfect while Mary was more interested in spending time with her guest. I used to wonder if Mary was just lazy and knew that she probably couldn't do anything to please Martha anyway, so she just opted to take a chair instead.

Up until the last couple of years, I've related very well with Martha. I understood her desire to keep all her plates spinning at the same time, priding herself in the fact that none of them crashed to the ground. I'm guessing she took great satisfaction in making sure everything was crossed off her list at the end of each day; and was very frustrated when it wasn't.

Mary, on the other hand, was someone with whom I couldn't relate at all. How in the world could she just sit there when she knew that there were potatoes to peel and bread to bake? Guests were coming! What would they think if they arrived and everything wasn't in order? How embarrassing! She really needed to get her priorities in order.

Then I began spending time in the oncology center with my mother-in-law. I started seeing people come in for their treatments who were pale, thin, and weak. Obviously their lives had come to a screeching halt, as they had to learn a new "normal": one that included many doctors' appointments, needles, and IVs. Things that used to seem important to them on a daily basis didn't seem so critical anymore.

Spending the hours that I have in this environment is changing me. While I still love to have a list to work from and look forward to crossing each task off, I'm starting to understand the importance of sitting still too.

While accomplishing my tasks still gives me a level of satisfaction, time spent with Mary's guest, my Lord Jesus Christ, is even more satisfying. Learning to be quiet, learning to just listen to His Word, is healing to my soul. I know that I have much to learn from my Jesus. If I'm always on the run, it will be difficult for me to absorb His ways. I'm learning that time spent with Him is never wasted. Those will never be moments I will regret.

We live in a crazy world with much chaos going on around us. As a result, it is easy to become too busy doing things with no eternal value. Because of this, it is critical that we grasp what is truly important. For us to look more like Christ, for us to be a light in the deep darkness, we must spend time at Jesus' feet, listening to what He has to teach us. Only then will we be equipped and able to lead others to His saving grace.

My Jesus Prayer

Jesus, forgive me for the times when I have thought my schedule was more important than sitting at Your feet. It's no wonder that my world has felt so chaotic at times because my eyes weren't focused on You. Help me show others that there is nothing more important in my life than You.

DAY 70

Being Prepared

Commit your actions to the Lord, and your plans will succeed (Proverbs 16:3).

It was the week before our daughter Megan would be entering the hospital to give birth to our second grandson. Knowing that life would be just a little more hectic now with two children in their home under the age of two, we had decided to spend a marathon day in her kitchen. Our goal? To have twenty-two dinners tucked away in her freezer before we collapsed!

We survived the day, barely. Both of us were fairly spent. As we finished up, Megan said, "I don't think I ever want to cook again in my life!" She had probably cut up more meat and vegetables in one day than she had in the past several months combined, and it had taken its toll. Standing for a day can be difficult for many of us, but being nine months pregnant made it even more taxing.

All that work would be worth it though in the weeks to come when she or her husband could go to the freezer and pull something out to put either in their crockpot or oven for dinner. The time that they would save from having to be in the kitchen could be spent with their precious children or possibly in taking a much needed nap. A little sacrifice that day would make for a lighter workload in the days to come.

What we accomplished that day is what I call being prepared. Anticipating very busy days in the future, it's good to figure out what can be done today in preparation for possibly stressful times ahead. It involves thinking ahead, making plans, and then working to get some of the tasks accomplished ahead of time to hopefully make life a little easier in the future.

I realize that circumstances don't always allow us to prepare for stressful, chaotic days. But I do think that there are times in our lives when some forethought would have prevented us from falling apart under our workload. I can think of times in my life where I have felt panicky and overwhelmed with the tasks at hand, but when I honestly evaluated why I felt as I did, it was often because I waited until the last minute instead of being prepared ahead of time.

I think that for some reason, we sometimes think that we look more spiritual if our schedule is packed day in and day out. We want people to think that we are so driven and so motivated to serve that we don't have even a moment to stop and be still. As we looked at Mary and Martha yesterday, we learned that not having our days completely filled can often be a good thing because it gives us time to learn from our Jesus. People might be more willing to listen to us talk about Him if they see that our schedules are well-planned and organized and centered around the One we claim to know.

Are there things in your future that have you stressed to the max? Take today's scripture to heart and commit those things to Him. Then see if there is something you can do today in preparation. You may not be able to take an entire day out of your schedule now, but even marking one thing off your to-do list will help to lower your blood pressure and help settle your nerves. The Lord promises to guide us in our plans, but I believe He wants us to do our part in using our time wisely as we plan.

Benjamin Franklin said, "By failing to prepare, you are preparing to fail." His words are wise. Start taking action today to move you closer to being prepared for the days to come, so that others will sense the peace in you that only Jesus can give.

My Jesus Prayer

Jesus, I know that my hectic schedule is often a result of not planning as I should. Help me to commit my plans to You and then follow Your leading to make the necessary preparations for my life.

LUANN GERIG FULTON

DAY 71

Perspectives

So we tell others about Christ, warning everyone and teaching everyone with all the wisdom God has given us. We want to present them to God, perfect in their relationship to Christ (Colossians 1:28).

The day finally arrived when we welcomed our new grandson, Ezekiel Daniel Yao, into our family. This blessed event confirmed in my mind that there is just nothing better than being a grandma!

After that wonderful day, I was thinking about the word *perspective*. Ezekiel weighed in at eight pounds, twelve ounces and was twenty-two inches long. For many, this sounded like a pretty good-sized baby, but to us, he seemed fairly small. The reason was that his brother, Elias, weighed a little over eleven pounds when he was born almost two years before. How a person looked at this depended on their perspective.

To help our daughter and son-in-law during that time, we kept our older grandson, Elias, the week after Ezekiel's arrival. Having a twenty-two-month-old in our home reminded me why we have our children when we are young. We absolutely loved having him stay with us, but it took a lot of energy to keep up with him. As I cared for him though, I realized how much my perspective had changed over the years. When my children were young, I was much more focused on making sure all the details in my home were covered and things were running smoothly. Now my perspective as to what needed to be accomplished while we are together had changed. I had now realized that there were very few things in this life that were more important than spending time with my grandchildren.

I also became another year older during that week. Some people may have thought I had one foot in the grave because I had turned fifty-six. But to some of the people I knew who were in their 80s and 90s, I was just a young whipper-snapper! It all had to do with their perspective.

Several days following Ezekiel's arrival, we had the privilege of worshipping with our church family. It was Easter Sunday. According to some people's perspective, it was a day to see the Easter Bunny and get lots of candy. The story of a risen King was just a fable to them, whereas we knew it to be the truth. Our perspective, or view, was that Christ gave His all, sacrificing Himself on a cross for our sins, after which He rose three days later so we could spend eternity with Him.

The week with my grandson reminded me that as I aged, my attitudes and viewpoints had changed due to my life experiences and (hopefully) my maturity level. I often hear people say, "If I had known then what I know now, things would have been different." Of course they would have been, but we don't have that option. And no matter what we would have known "then," we would still see things differently now.

It is impossible for us to change our past, but we can look at our present as we prepare for our future. The question is this: Are our perspectives changing for the better as we age and mature, or have we allowed the world to change our perspectives by drawing us down to its level? Are we consumed with the "what-if's" and "should-haves" of our past, displaying only negativity to those we meet, or are we progressing and moving closer to look more and more like our Jesus? Are our perspectives based on biblical truths or just fables and hearsay?

As we go through our day, let's spend some time evaluating our perspectives. Are they bringing glory to Him and drawing others closer to the risen King or are our views so much like the world that no one would know we are a child of this King? The world is in desperate need to see Jesus "with skin on," not just clones of themselves. It is our responsibility to make sure we tell them about our Jesus as we point them to the King of Kings and Lord of Lords.

LUANN GERIG FULTON

My Jesus Prayer

> *Jesus, help me base my beliefs on Your Word and not on my own perspectives. The Bible is filled with absolute truths that I need to be sharing with those with whom I meet today. Adjust my ideas until they match up with Yours. Make me like You, Lord.*

DAY 72
Thinking Like Jesus

Don't copy the behavior and customs of this world, but let God transform you into a new person by changing the way you think. Then you will learn to know God's will for you, which is good and pleasing and perfect (Romans 12:2).

I live in Indiana and it never ceases to amaze me how changeable our weather can be in just a few days. We can go from snow flurries to seventy degrees in a forty-eight-hour period, especially in the spring. If we get a day when we have sun and warmth without high winds, we are thrilled. After an Indiana winter, this kind of day is welcomed. When those days come, I find that my energy level is higher, my mood is cheerier, and my outlook on life is so much more positive than it had been before, and all because the weather cooperated!

I'm smart enough to know (and I've been a Christian long enough to know) that it shouldn't be that way. It shouldn't take flawless weather to make me a nicer, more productive person. I should behave as Christ would whether the sun is shining or we are getting a blizzard. But I don't always live up to what I know to be true.

The problem is that I don't always think like Jesus. It's not that I don't know how He would respond in different situations, because I do; I just choose to respond *my* way. Someone doesn't treat me like I think I should be treated and I can be quick to react unkindly instead of answering with love. I see someone who doesn't look like I think they should look and I can be quick to judge without ever finding out their "story." I can hear of blessings that someone else has received and I sometimes ooze jealousy instead of rejoicing with those who rejoice.

Unfortunately, I don't think I'm alone. At different times in my life I've heard stories about people not getting along with friends or family members. I remember asking a woman once if she had any siblings and her face turned to stone. She proceeded to tell me that she had one sister but they hadn't spoken in years, all because of a very small misunderstanding. Years had been lost—wasted—because neither of them was willing to think like Jesus.

I've seen long-lasting friendships disintegrate because of words spoken in haste. Instead of making the effort to hear each other out and making the choice to forgive and show love, a wedge had been driven into the relationship and neither person was willing to act like Jesus.

The saddest thing is that many of these people were Christians just like me. All of us know how Jesus would act and respond, but at times each of us has chosen to respond our way instead of His. It all comes down to whether we are willing to follow Christ's lead and allow Him to shape us so that our thoughts are the same as His.

I believe I'm going to commit to saying a certain prayer today that won't be based on the weather or the world swirling around me. It won't be a long speech with flowery language; it will just be these simple words, "Jesus, mold me and shape me until I think like You." Would you be willing to join me? I just have a sneaking suspicion that He will enjoy hearing our short prayer and will be very happy to answer it.

My **Jesus Prayer**

Jesus, mold me and shape me until I think like You.

DAY 73

Memories to Ponder

Every time I think of you, I give thanks to my God
(Philippians 1:3).

I had been working on notes for speaking engagements that were coming up. It never ceases to amaze me how God will suddenly take me on a detour while I'm studying, to either teach me something new or remind me of something I may be neglecting.

As I was researching, I came across verses in the Bible that I have read many, many times. But when I read them this time, God gave me a new perspective. The verses included our scripture for today. In Philippians 1:3-6, Paul was talking about the Christians in Philippi when he said, *"Every time I think of you, I give thanks to my God. Whenever I pray, I make my requests for all of you with joy, for you have been my partners in spreading the Good News about Christ from the time you first heard it until now. And I am certain that God, who began the good work within you, will continue his work until it is finally finished on the day when Christ Jesus returns."*

As I read these words, this thought came to me: *Do I ever think about what memories I give to other people?* These Christians in Philippi had given Paul such good memories because they had been so supportive and involved in his life. How amazing that he could say that every time he thought of them, he thanked God for them! I wonder if that is how people think when they have thoughts about me. Or have the memories that I have made with other people been negative ones? When they think of me, are their thoughts about how bitter I was or how negative I was while we were together? Or do they have memories that bring them joy and thankfulness for the time they spent with me?

As I've shared before, the world we are living in seems to be coming more unhinged every day. It's easy to fall into the trap of being negative with our words and actions. It's also easy to whine and complain when we are around others, failing to share the joy of the Lord that is supposed to be in our hearts. It's sobering when we think that there are unsaved people listening to us go on and on about everything that's wrong in our lives, and we never tell them about what Jesus has done for us. It's no wonder many of them don't want what we have. We don't sound any better off than they are!

Notice that Paul stated that these Christians had been partners with him in spreading the good news. He didn't say that they had been sharing their complaints, their worries, and their gossip with him. We have good news that needs to be shared from now until Jesus returns, and the Christians in Philippi understood this.

Yes, the world we live in is pretty chaotic, but I think we make it even worse by not keeping our focus on Christ. He has done great things for us and He is the One who will be victorious in the end. Our job, while still on this earth, is to make sure that others see Him through us, so every time they think of us they will think of Him. That, my friend, should give them good memories to ponder.

Remember, when our story becomes His story, people will be drawn to us and they will have precious memories of our Savior *and* us.

My Jesus Prayer

*Jesus, when others remember me, I want them
to think of You. Help me put my desires aside,
concentrating on how You want me to live so that will
be accomplished.*

DAY 74

The Small "Talk Box"

In those days when you pray, I will listen (Jeremiah 29:12).

I was thinking one day about the olden days when we didn't have cell phones. We used to set our answering machine when we left home (that is, if we remembered to) and we checked it when we returned. In the meantime, no one could get ahold of us unless they somehow physically tracked us down. People just understood that they would have to wait for us to call them back once we listened to their message.

I remember when my husband first said that he thought we should get a cell phone. Since we owned a mobile catering service, he felt it would be a huge asset to have one in case he or one of our employees needed help while they were on the road. I was dead set against it. While I agreed with his logic, all I could envision was being constantly interrupted when we weren't at home. Our home phone rang often because our business line also rang in our house. The last thing I wanted was to have to listen to more ringing when we were gone.

I eventually gave in and we purchased our first cell phone. It was huge and the reception wasn't the best, but we had finally entered the mobile world. I soon realized what an asset it was to those in our business, and it wasn't long before we had quite a few cell phones on our plan. And yes, the day finally arrived when I had my very own mobile device.

If we fast forward quite a few years, I now feel lost if I don't have my cell phone with me. I'm so used to carrying it that when I do forget it at home, I'm always wondering if someone is trying to call or text me and waiting for my answer. Honestly, I am *way* too dependent on that phone and I need to work hard on loosening my grip on it.

I read a sign one day that said, "The first ever cordless phone was created by God. He named it *prayer*. It never loses its signal and you never have to recharge it. You can use it anywhere!" At first this made me chuckle and then it made me think. I started asking myself if I was as diligent in making sure my prayer life was always connected as I was about making sure my cell phone was charged and ready for use. I check my phone often to make sure the battery will get me through the day, but it is easy to forget that my true Power Source, Jesus, never needs to be charged and can never be misplaced or left behind. He is always available, never "out of area," and never even needs an upgrade! I can always stay plugged in to His power, seven days a week, twenty-four hours a day. He is willing to communicate with me every day and every hour. I never get a busy signal or have to leave a message. It blows my mind to think that the Creator of the universe wants to be in continual conversation with me!

Why would I not want to tell others about this Power Source of mine? I have no problem telling others about my latest cell phone upgrade, so I should be even more excited to tell others about my Jesus!

I wonder what would happen today if every time I reached for my phone, I stopped and breathed a prayer of gratitude to God for His power that He makes available to me. I wonder if it would help me keep my focus on Him when life seems to be swirling around me. If nothing else, maybe it would help remind me that He is always the constant in my life. He is the One who never changes and is always available to recharge me, instead of me needing to recharge Him. And maybe, just maybe, it would help me be much more intent on keeping the lines of communication open with Him, instead of relying so heavily on the small "talk box" in my pocket.

My Jesus Prayer

> *Jesus, I am so thankful that You are always with me,*
> *that I never get a busy signal, and that You never run*
> *out of power. Help me today to recharge, using Your*
> *constant and ever-present connection!*

DAY 75

Rest...Now?

"If it is true that you look favorably on me, let me know your ways so I may understand you more fully and continue to enjoy your favor. And remember that this nation is your very own people." The Lord replied, "I will personally go with you, Moses, and I will give you rest—everything will be fine for you" (Exodus 33:13-14).

I don't know about you, but I just love it (tongue-in-cheek) when I start a week with my calendar set and then something happens to change everything. Not just one day's plans or two, but absolutely everything.

We were heading home on a Monday evening after visiting my dad and I made the comment to Dan that my throat was a little sore. Thinking that's all it was, I swallowed some vitamin C before bed and thought that would be the end of it. I woke up Tuesday morning feeling like a truck had run over me and wasn't able to accomplish anything that day.

I decided Wednesday morning that I better see my doctor because surely she could just prescribe something that would make everything better and I could get back to my schedule. Unfortunately, she wasn't too concerned with my schedule. She checked me over and said that I had a virus that was rampant right then and that there wasn't a quick fix. She even had the audacity to tell me that I was probably going to get worse before I got better. Such encouraging words.

After giving me something to, hopefully, settle down my cough and help me sleep, she informed me that the best thing I could do was go home and go to bed for two to three days. She said I needed rest and lots of it. I remember thinking that there was no way I was going to stay down that long. I just had too much to do. Oh, when will I learn?

By the following Monday I still hadn't been out of the house since my doctor's appointment the week before. Very little on my calendar had been accomplished during that week and I couldn't even go to church on Sunday. That nasty "bug" hit me hard, zapping me of my energy and forcing me to go through with my doctor's orders. Each day I got up thinking of things that I would attempt to achieve that day, but soon realized that most would remain undone.

It's funny how when I'm healthy and going strong, I often wish I had a day to just rest, but then when I don't have any other choice but to rest, I'm not happy. Why? Because no one wants to have to rest because they are sick. It's one thing if it is our choice to take a day off, but another if we are forced to rest.

When I think of those whose health deters them every day from doing what they would love to do, I feel ashamed that I whine when I have to be down for only a week. Mine was just a short-term inconvenience, but there are many who have encountered a huge detour in their life and find themselves on a journey they surely didn't have on their schedule. Day after day, week after week, and sometimes month after month, they face health issues that prohibit them from fulfilling their dreams. Yet so many of them have made the choice to use their unplanned circumstances to shine their light for their Jesus. They are determined to not dwell on what they *can't* do, but on what they *can* do to touch the lives of others.

We see in our scripture today that Moses wanted to understand the Lord and His ways more fully. The Lord promised him that He would be with him every step of the way and that everything would be fine. He also told Moses that He would give him rest. I don't think the Lord was just talking about the fact that Moses and his people could rest once they reached the Promised Land. I think He was telling him that *His* presence would give him rest—physically, mentally, and spiritually—no matter what life threw at him.

And the same is true for us. The Lord's presence within us can give us rest when an unexpected detour comes our way. Rest when our spirit feels unsettled and unsatisfied. Rest when the world around us is in disarray. Rest when we are apprehensive about our future. Rest when our mind wants to dwell on our past. Rest when His plans don't concur with our plans.

Are you in need of rest today—physically, mentally, or spiritually? The Lord promises that His presence can give you the kind of rest you need for today, tomorrow, and the weeks and months to come. He knows absolutely everything about you and nothing that you are going through is a surprise to Him. Today may not be the day you had planned on your calendar, but if you seek Him, He promises to walk with you every step of the way and give you rest. I can't think of anyone that could be a better walking partner than Him!

My Jesus Prayer

Jesus, what transpires today may not be on my agenda, but I know it will be on Yours. Walk with me and guide me wherever You want me to go.

LUANN GERIG FULTON

DAY 76
Worth The Cost

And so, dear brothers and sisters, I plead with you to give your bodies to God because of all he has done for you. Let them be a living and holy sacrifice – the kind he will find acceptable. This is truly the way to worship him. Don't copy the behavior and customs of this world, but let God transform you into a new person by changing the way you think. Then you will learn to know God's will for you, which is good and pleasing and perfect (Romans 12:1-2).

I have a confession to make. I don't like to shop. There, I've gotten that out in the open. When I've shared that tidbit of information with people in the past, especially other women, they have often looked at me like I had horns. I know, I'm not a normal woman. It is torture for me to have to go on a quest for items to buy. I can think of many other things that I would rather be doing than shopping—any kind of shopping—but especially clothes shopping.

As a result, you won't often see me in a variety of outfits. If I find something I like, I usually wear it until it isn't wearable (much to the chagrin of my children and sometimes even my husband). Unfortunately though, clothes don't last forever, so the day eventually comes when new items are needed and I have to push myself to visit establishments that sell clothing.

When I returned home from one of these dreaded excursions I realized that it was time to clean out my closet and get rid of those items that were past their prime. I'm smart enough to know that if those gems are left in my closet, I will resort to wearing the old tried and true garments that have served me so well. My husband teases me that I still have clothes that I wore in junior high. Oh, how I wish that were true because it would mean I am still the same size as I was back then, but regrettably, I am not.

To be truthful, I think I am this way about shopping because I don't like change. If my clothes are comfortable and still cover the parts of my body that need covered, I'm fine, even if they aren't the latest fashion. I'm the same way in my home. Until recently when we did some remodeling, I had had the same pictures and decorations on my walls for years. I like things to stay the same, and having to push myself out of my comfort zone to make changes just didn't make me feel comfortable.

Unfortunately, we are living in a rapidly changing world. I don't like that either. I want things to be as they were years ago when God was still someone that most people believed in and revered. Sadly, the day is here when it isn't only the soldiers that serve our country who need to be brave, but us Christians also need to be brave. Our religious freedoms are being taken away, and we need to be willing to stand up for what we know to be the truths given to us by our Lord and Savior. It will not be easy and it won't be the popular thing to do, but it is what we have been called to do.

To be willing to stand up for what I know to be truth means I will have to make changes. I will have to be willing to step out of my comfort zone to do whatever God calls me to do to reach as many people as I can for Him. I can't just sit around and enjoy being comfortable while I hope someone else is loving, caring, and sharing with others about their Jesus.

There is a quote from Charles Spurgeon that really speaks to me, "If sinners be damned, at least let them leap to Hell [sic] over our dead bodies. And if they perish, let them perish with our arms wrapped about their knees, imploring them to stay. If Hell [sic] must be filled, let it be filled in the teeth of our exertions, and let not one go unwarned and unprayed for." I don't know about you, but this is something I want said of me. I want to be willing to sacrifice, whatever the cost, to make sure those with whom I come in contact don't spend their eternity in hell. If my loved one was heading toward something on this earth that I knew was going to deeply hurt them, I know I would do everything in my power to stop them from going in that direction. I wouldn't care how I looked or what I would have to give up or how much I would have to change my lifestyle to keep them safe. It would be worth whatever the cost.

How much more urgent should our actions be when we know that many around us have not accepted Jesus Christ as their Savior? They will not just experience pain on this earth, but they will spend eternity in hell. We have to do everything we can, imploring them to accept Him while they still can. Time is short and the cost is high, and our comfort shouldn't be our focus. I firmly believe it will be worth the cost!

My Jesus Prayer

Jesus, I know that our time is short on this earth and I need to be willing to stand up for You. Give me the courage to make the necessary changes to tell everyone I see about my Jesus.

DAY 77

Imperfect People

Let us think of ways to motivate one another to acts of love and good works. And let us not neglect our meeting together, as some people do, but encourage one another, especially now that the day of his return is drawing near (Hebrews 10:24-25).

I love Sundays. I know many people spend their week counting the hours until Friday rolls around, but I'm that way with Sunday. When one Sunday is over, I can't wait until the next weekend when we get to be in the Lord's house once again. I am blessed to attend a church where you can feel the Holy Spirit working each and every Sunday; it makes me wish there was more than one Sunday each week.

I usually wake up on this day of rest anxious to get to church. I rarely have trouble getting out of bed and hitting the shower because I know where I'm headed. The same was true one Sunday morning as I prepared to make the trek to our church, but when I opened up God's Word to read my devotions before we left, I was hit with these heartwarming words from Ecclesiastes 1: *These are the words of the Teacher, King David's son, who ruled in Jerusalem.*

> *"Everything is meaningless," says the Teacher, "completely meaningless!"*
>
> *What do people get for all their hard work under the sun? Generations come and generations go, but the earth never changes. The sun rises and the sun sets, then hurries around to rise again. The wind blows south, and then turns north. Around and around it goes, blowing in circles. Rivers run into the sea, but the sea is never full. Then the water returns again to the rivers and flows out again to the sea. Everything is wearisome beyond description. No matter how much we*

see, we are never satisfied. No matter how much we hear, we are not content.

History merely repeats itself. It has all been done before. Nothing under the sun is truly new. Sometimes people say, "Here is something new!" But actually it is old; nothing is ever truly new. We don't remember what happened in the past, and in future generations, no one will remember what we are doing now.

I, the Teacher, was king of Israel, and I lived in Jerusalem. I devoted myself to search for understanding and to explore by wisdom everything being done under heaven. I soon discovered that God has dealt a tragic existence to the human race. I observed everything going on under the sun, and really, it is all meaningless — like chasing the wind.

What is wrong cannot be made right. What is missing cannot be recovered.

I said to myself, "Look, I am wiser than any of the kings who ruled in Jerusalem before me. I have greater wisdom and knowledge than any of them." So I set out to learn everything from wisdom to madness and folly. But I learned firsthand that pursuing all this is like chasing the wind.

The greater my wisdom, the greater my grief.

To increase knowledge only increases sorrow (Ecclesiastes 1).

Well now, that was uplifting! Believe me when I say that this negative theme only got worse as I continued through Ecclesiastes. To say it was depressing is an understatement. They sure weren't words to fill me with inspiration as I headed off to worship God.

They were words though to remind me that not everyone got up that morning thrilled to be going to church. Some, I'm sure, dreaded getting up because they knew they *had* to go to a service where they haven't felt the Spirit working in years. There is a good chance that others woke up and had no intention of going to the Lord's house because of pain that had been inflicted on them from those who called themselves Christians.

More than likely, there were others who got out of bed and never gave church a thought because they had never darkened the door.

I believe many people feel that life is futile just as Solomon did in Ecclesiastes. There is so much evil going on in this world that it is easy for people to feel like giving up. Life just keeps knocking them down over and over; it's hard for them to see a silver lining in any cloud. Day after day plays out just like the day before and it takes everything they have just to put one foot in front of another.

If you are feeling like this today, please allow me to give you some advice. First of all, if you are attending a church that isn't Bible-based and prayer-focused, I urge you to do whatever you can to share with those you know that church is more than a social club. Life is too short and Christ's return is on the horizon. We dare not just "play church."

If you aren't attending church because you have been hurt from those in the church, I am deeply sorry. My heart breaks for those who have walked out the door, vowing they would never return. Unfortunately, those of us in the church are far from perfect and sometimes our actions or words are not done or said in love. I implore you to give worshipping on Sunday another chance. There are many churches out there, although filled with imperfect people that will love you and want to walk on your journey with you.

If by chance you are reading this and you have never tried church on a Sunday, why not give it a try? You may have heard some negative and hopefully a lot of positive things about becoming involved with others in your community to worship the One who created you. Maybe it's time for you to find out for yourself what actually transpires on a Sunday morning in a local congregation.

Yes, life can seem like it is just as meaningless as Solomon said at times. But I'm here to share with you today that there is more to life than that. It's hard to put into words, but the time I spend in worship helps me exponentially throughout the week. It gives me hope, keeps me focused, and inspires me to reach out and make a difference in the lives of those around me.

I would love for you to wake up on Sunday mornings as excited as I am to walk through the doors of a local church. Warning: You won't find anyplace that is filled with perfect people, but I know there are many imperfect people who want to "do life" with you. You don't have to walk your journey alone.

My Jesus Prayer

Jesus, I am so thankful that it was Your design for us to meet together for worship with our brothers and sisters. Help me, Father, to seek out a place that is filled with Your Spirit so we can learn Your ways together.

DAY 78
Newborns

And now, just as you accepted Christ Jesus as your Lord, you must continue to follow him. Let your roots grow down into him, and let your lives be built on him. Then your faith will grow strong in the truth you were taught, and you will overflow with thankfulness (Colossians 2:6-7).

The days were filled with expectation in our family as we anxiously awaited the arrival of our first granddaughter, Emma. Even though I hadn't met her yet, I knew that when she finally made her appearance, she wouldn't be able to crawl, or walk, or talk in words that were understandable. I knew she would cry at times when her parents wished she wouldn't and wouldn't sleep when they wished she would. She wouldn't be ready to eat Grandma's cooking and, believe it or not, she wouldn't even be potty trained!

None of these things though, would dampen my love for our precious Emma. I wouldn't be upset with her when I held her for the first time, telling her how disappointed I was in her because she hadn't mastered these skills. The reason was because I didn't expect her to be able to do any of those things. She would be a newborn, and anyone with any intelligence would know that a newborn baby isn't ready to crawl or walk or do the other things I listed. Those things would come, but it would take time while her body and mind grew and she developed into the young person that God intended her to be.

Why is it then that when a person makes the awesome decision to accept Jesus Christ as their personal Lord and Savior, we think they should immediately look, act, and speak like a fully developed Christian? They are babes in Christ, just like a newborn baby! It may be too much for them to even crawl in their walk at the beginning, but in time they will crawl, walk, and even run on their journey. They may cry and say things that we wish they wouldn't, and they won't make decisions like we wish they would. We shouldn't expect them to, nor should we tell them how disappointed we are in them because they don't have everything in their life cleaned up.

Our wait was finally over when Emma Christine joined our family on July 22nd, weighing six pounds, ten ounces and measuring twenty-one inches long. She was absolutely perfect with blonde hair and beautiful blue eyes. On the day of her arrival I discovered that I was right; she couldn't do any of the things that an adult or even an older child could do. But the things she couldn't do didn't even cross my mind because I was instantly, completely, and totally in love with this precious granddaughter of ours. I loved her enough to allow her time to grow and develop at her own pace.

That is exactly what Emma has done over the past year. She has learned to smile, roll over, laugh, crawl, and will soon be walking. Her fun personality has blossomed as she has developed at her own pace. I knew that she would change and grow in God's timing, just like babes in Christ.

Isn't it amazing that we want grace from others for ourselves, but fail to extend grace to those around us? Let's remember that we are all a work in progress and that those who are newborns need to feel and see our love, regardless of what stage of development they are in. Those times of growth will come for them and for us, but it will take time while our faith grows and we develop into the faithful followers that God intends us to be.

My Jesus Prayer

Jesus, help me to extend grace to those who are just beginning their journey with You. I need to keep in mind that they will grow and develop in their walk in Your timing, not mine.

DAY 79

Hand in Hand

No, O people, the Lord has told you what is good, and this is what he requires of you: to do what is right, to love mercy, and to walk humbly with your God (Micah 6:8).

I have learned so much since I have taken on the role of being a grandma. People told me that it would be wonderful and that it would help me grow as a person, but I couldn't completely grasp how great it would be until I held our first grandson. He totally stole my heart and then his brother did the same thing less than two years later, followed by our precious granddaughter.

One of the things that makes my heart melt is when one of them takes my hand when we are walking together. It's a very simple gesture, but I feel emotional every time they do it. There is something about having that small hand in mine that makes me feel incredibly blessed that I am able to have a part in their life. I don't take that opportunity lightly. I want to spend as much time with each one of them as I can, building a relationship that will last a lifetime.

The practical positive of being hand in hand with them is that I am assured they are by my side. As with most youngsters, their legs often want to take them where they shouldn't go, so if I have their hand I have more control of their path. Even though they may not always think that is a good thing, I know it is in their best interest to stay by my side.

I was thinking about this recently when I was reading Amos 3:3. It asks the question, *"Can two people walk together without agreeing on the direction?"* Of course this is a rhetorical question that is easy to answer. There is no way two people can walk hand in hand and go in two different directions. It's just not possible.

This is applicable to our walk with Christ. If we are going to go on the path that He has planned for us, we must be willing to walk with Him hand in hand. When we let go and think we can walk on our own, problems usually begin to arise and we start to lose our way. We need to realize that even when we don't feel like walking with Him, it is imperative that we do it anyway, because it is always in our best interest to stay by His side.

I just can't help but believe that Christ also gets emotional when we want to take His hand and walk with Him. He loves us so much and wants to continually work on our relationship with Him: one that will last beyond our lifetime. I know how much I love my children and grandchildren, but that doesn't hold a candle to the love that my heavenly Father has for me. I don't know about you, but that thought gives me chills, makes me feel greatly favored, and makes me never want to let go of His hand.

My Jesus Prayer

> *Jesus, how precious it is to know that You want to walk hand in hand with me. Hold my hand tight, Lord, because I never want to wander away from Your presence.*

ASK ME ABOUT MY JESUS

DAY 80
Charging Station

Now all glory to God, who is able, through his mighty power at work within us, to accomplish infinitely more than we might ask or think. Glory to him in the church and in Christ Jesus through all generations forever and ever! Amen (Ephesians 3:20-21).

I am a sweeper-a-holic. I can let other things go in my home and it doesn't bother me, but having an unswept carpet drives me nuts!

The problem lies in the fact that because I've endured four back surgeries, I have been told that I shouldn't push a vacuum anymore. That may be news to cheer about for you, but this woman didn't like those words from her surgeon. I tried really hard to continue sweeping and I did my best to carefully push the machine forward and backward so that it wouldn't cause me pain. Unfortunately, each instance of disobedience quickly reminded me why my doctor had given those orders.

We finally decided to purchase a robotic sweeper. In case you aren't familiar with this gizmo, it is a vacuum that runs all by itself. I can either schedule it to run at a certain time, or I can just push the button and it takes off on its own. It moves away from its charging station, lasers the surrounding area so that it knows where to clean, and then gets to work.

The only negative is that it can't sweep my entire home without having to recharge itself part way through. Fortunately though, if it needs more power, it automatically returns to the charging base and powers up. While it is recharging, I usually empty its dirt bin so that it will be ready for the next leg of its job. Once it is recharged, it goes back to sweeping the carpet right where it left off, all on its own with no help from me.

I've decided that I need to learn from my sweeper. When I find myself feeling drained physically, mentally or spiritually, I often simply try harder. I dig my heels in and think that if I just work harder or put in longer days, I'll be able to be the person God wants me to be. The problem with this theory is that, of course, I run out of steam and I get so drained that I'm not productive at all. If I'm honest, I would have to admit that it is at those times that I have probably let go of Christ's hand and tried to venture off on my own. That's when frustration and despair can rear their ugly heads. There is no way that others are seeing Jesus in me then.

I need to realize that when I've used up all my power, there is Someone who is waiting for me to remember that I need *His* power to do what I've been called to do. It is critical that I take the time to plug into Jesus and allow Him to recharge and refuel me for the tasks ahead. It's during that time of empowerment that He is able to clean every crevice of my being, wiping away every bit of dirt and grime that I have picked up while in the world.

Are you feeling drained and powerless as you begin your day? Maybe it's time you returned to the ultimate "charging station": Jesus Christ. He already knows exactly what you will face today and in the days to come and has already "lasered out" a plan that is perfect for you. He will be able to cleanse all the dirt that has crept into your life and replace it with His sweet Spirit. His Spirit will refuel and fill you with the power you need to follow His plan, and as a result others will see His image in you.

My Jesus Prayer

Jesus, it is easy to become weary when I rely on my own power. Thank You for always being ready and willing to recharge me and cleanse me anew. Help me to plug in to You today.

DAY 81

He's Watching Me

And the very hairs on your head are all numbered. So don't be afraid; you are more valuable to God than a whole flock of sparrows (Luke 12:7).

I love to listen to Christian music as I walk early in the morning because it lifts my spirit and makes the time go faster as I exercise. A song came on one day that immediately propelled my thoughts to a day years ago that I often recall.

On that day, I was sitting in a hospital room next to my mother's bed. She was restless and confused. As a result of Alzheimer's, her mind didn't always comprehend what was going on around her and being in an unfamiliar place made it even worse for her. I remember talking to her and trying to calm her, but I wasn't having much success.

All of a sudden, she began to relax and I saw her beautiful smile return. She looked at me and said, "Do you hear that? Do you hear that singing? It's beautiful!" All I could hear were ordinary hospital noises, but I wasn't about to let on to her that I couldn't perceive what she could.

I decided that because whatever she could hear was calming her, I would play along. I told her that I could barely hear the singing and I just couldn't make out the words and wondered if she could tell me what they said. Her response? "Oh, they are singing my favorite song, His Eye is On the Sparrow. Isn't it beautiful?"

By this time, her face was beaming and she was completely relaxed. We sat there together, Mom being ministered to by her Savior and me being ministered to by my mother. I believe that the Lord knew what words my mom needed to hear to remind her of His constant care. I, in turn, needed to see once again the deep, powerful, and intimate relationship she had with her heavenly Father. Her faith was so deep that even in the darkness of Alzheimer's, she could still recall the promises of her Savior. During her life, my mom didn't just talk about her faith, she lived her faith day in and day out, even at times when following Him meant she had to sacrifice. She was willing to give and do whatever her Lord asked of her.

That's the kind of relationship I want to have with the Lord. I want His words, His wisdom, and His promises to be so much a part of me that no matter what happens I will be able to draw from His power. But I realize that that doesn't just happen. It isn't something that is just automatically in me because I had Christian parents and grandparents, and it doesn't even come as a result of sitting in church every Sunday. Just like sitting in a garage doesn't make me a car, sitting in a church doesn't automatically make me a devoted follower of Christ. I have to be willing and open to learn from those who have walked with their Savior longer than me, and from my brothers and sisters in Christ with whom I worship. Ultimately, my bond with the Lord happens over time as I fellowship with Him, reading His Word, and listening and sharing through prayer.

Just as those words from my mom's favorite song were a comfort to her during her hospital stay, they are a comfort to me today, knowing that nothing will happen to me that He won't see. The One who knows everything wants to have an intimate, personal relationship with me, and it is my choice how close I will allow Him to be. I have no reason to be discouraged or lonely because Jesus is all I need and He promises to be my constant friend. Oh, what a comfort that is to my soul!

My Jesus Prayer

> *Jesus, I know that no one else can take responsibility for my relationship with You. I have to be willing to surrender my life and then make it a priority to spend time learning and growing with You. Thank you so much, Jesus, for being my constant and faithful friend.*

DAY 82

Choosing To Laugh

These are just the beginning of all that he does, merely a whisper of his power. Who, then, can comprehend the thunder of his power? (Job 26:14).

I make it a goal to read the whole Bible through each year, and I have to admit that I am always pretty excited when I finally arrive in the New Testament. I know there are many things to learn by reading the Old Testament, but I am always eager to begin reading about the arrival of baby Jesus and everything that transpired as He walked the earth.

I am always struck by the many miracles that Jesus performed. Time and time again He did the unbelievable. From turning water into wine to healing the lame, Jesus amazed everyone He met. Oh how wonderful it would have been to be there and actually see His ability to take the most desperate situation and turn it into a victory.

It's so easy for me, though, to read those accounts of His life and think that those kinds of miracles only happened back in "those days." I can easily fall into the trap of thinking that they were reserved for only those people who walked with Him when He was physically here. Sure, Christ had the power to handle any situation that came up back then, but again, that's because it was during biblical times. We are now many years past that and life is much harder than it was two thousand years ago, so we can't expect Him to be able to work in our lives the way He did for our ancestors back in the olden days.

You may laugh at my thinking, but this must be what is rattling around in my brain because, if I'm honest, there are many times when my actions prove this to be true. When I face a difficult situation, I stress out. When my life takes an unexpected detour, I freak out. When my health has a "hiccup," I spaz out. Time and time again, I show by my actions that I don't believe I serve a Savior who is able to handle anything that comes my way.

How many times do I look at something I am facing and act as though it is too big for even God to handle? Unfortunately, way too often. Instead of keeping my eyes on Him and resting in His power, strength, and ability to do more than I can even imagine, I succumb to Satan's lie that my circumstances are just too much for God to handle. It's hard to admit it, but it is true.

I saw a sign one time that said, "When I worry, I go to the mirror and say to myself, 'This tremendous thing that worries me is beyond solution. It is even too big for God.' Then I have a good laugh." I have asked God to sear these words in my mind so that when I am tempted to react as if He isn't able to handle my life, I will learn to laugh. It is so absurd to think that the One who created the universe, healed the blind, healed the lame, and raised the dead can't handle what life throws at me. Yes, it's absolutely ridiculous to think that way. So today, I will choose to laugh.

Are you facing something today that you think is just too big for God to handle? Think again, and laugh!

My Jesus Prayer

> *Jesus, why do I ever doubt Your ability and power to handle my circumstances? You have proved over and over that You can handle anything that I face. When I have doubts, help me to think again, and laugh!*

DAY 83

Change Begins at Home

And you must commit yourselves wholeheartedly to these commands that I am giving you today. Repeat them again and again to your children. Talk about them when you are at home and when you are on the road, when you are going to bed and when you are getting up. Tie them to your hands and wear them on your forehead as reminders. Write them on the doorposts of your house and on your gates (Deuteronomy 6:6-9).

I was reminded one day that what I say and how I act is often watched by others. Our grandson, Elias, who was two at the time, was staying with us for a few days, and it didn't take long to realize that he was always listening to what we said and watching what we did.

We were watching a game show together and one of the contestants solved a puzzle with only two letters showing. I immediately looked at my husband, and said, "How did she *do* that?" He, of course, had no clue how she did it either and we continued to watch the show.

We were so surprised then when after the next puzzle was solved, Elias said, "Grandma, how did she *do* that?" using the same exact inflection in his voice that I had used, putting an emphases on the word *do*. I looked over at him and it was obvious that he was quite proud of himself for talking just like the grownups.

It's cute when he copies something I say or do, most of the time. But I'm confident that there will be times when it won't be so cute. He is watching my every move and hearing my every word, and I'm pretty sure they won't always have a positive effect on him. He is a very smart little boy, and I'm guessing that he believes if Grandma behaves in a certain way, it is fine for him to do the same.

I have heard and read a lot in the media about making sure our children know what is acceptable and what isn't acceptable. Many have written articles about how they want to make sure their children know what kind of speech and behavior is appropriate, and I couldn't agree more. What bothers me, though, is that many of us are quick to point out the bad behavior of others to our children but we fail to make sure that our own behavior is what it should be.

Our children and grandchildren are often much smarter than we give them credit. What will they think if they hear us telling them not to mimic others, while we are not speaking or living as we ought. We can talk all day about how they should respect their bodies and not allow others to degrade them, but are they getting mixed messages when we are first in line to purchase the latest sordid book? How much will it confuse them if we tell them one thing, but then spend our Saturday night at the latest R-rated movie that is filled with sexual content? Probably the most sobering question is: How can we tell our children about their worth in God's eyes, but then condone the killing of innocent babies before they've even had the opportunity to take their first breath?

So much is going on around us in the world today that is completely out of our control, and it is having a huge influence on our children. Because of this, it is critical that what they see us *doing* doesn't conflict with what they hear us *saying*. If we tell them that having a relationship with Christ should be our main focus, then they need to see us making it a priority in our own lives. If they see that we are too busy to spend time daily with Him or that attending a sporting event or going to the lake often takes precedence over being in church on Sunday, our words won't have much impact. If they hear us saying that they need to choose their words wisely but hear us gossiping and using foul or vulgar talk, we might as well not share our words of "wisdom" with them at all. And if we tell them that Jesus loves the little children and that they are precious in His sight, we better be willing to do whatever we can to stop the murder of unborn, innocent lives because they are an "inconvenience" in our lives.

Changing our world begins at home, but if our children are receiving mixed messages from us, how can we expect them to make the right choices and live a life that is pleasing to the Lord? They must see Him in us first: in our words *and* in our actions. May God help us have the courage to make sure what we do is in line with what we say.

My Jesus Prayer

Jesus, help me to remember that I am always being watched, whether it be by my children, coworkers, friends, or neighbors. Help me to be a shining example of You so that if someone mimics me, what they do will be in line with Your Word.

LUANN GERIG FULTON

DAY 84
Blessed and Doubly Blessed

This is my commandment: Love each other in the same way I have loved you (John 15:12).

I am blessed. In fact I am blessed way more than I deserve and it seems like when doubt starts to rear its ugly head in me, God lovingly reminds me once again that I. Am. Blessed.

Let me explain. We are in a Connection Group from our church. You may have heard them referred to as small groups or cell groups, but we just have a fancier name for them. We are in this group with five other couples and we meet every other Wednesday evening. We share a snack together, share our praises and prayer concerns, and then spend time studying the Bible together. We even decided to tackle studying the book of Revelation together, and while I was a little apprehensive at the beginning, I loved it!

To be honest, I think we could do a study on "How to Buy Prunes" and I would be blessed. Why? Because we do life together. The twelve of us really care for each other and I'm confident that they look forward to being together as much as Dan and I do. These dear souls are our brothers and sisters in Christ and something special happens when we are together. During our evenings we have laughed and cried and shared, and as a result God has blessed us again and again.

I love our prayer time because it really helps draw us even closer. During this time we praise God for His answers to our prayers and we share those areas of our lives that still need God to work in a mighty way. We have seen Him do some amazing things as a result of our prayers, which is a wonderful reminder that our God is alive and well and more powerful than we can even imagine!

One of the things we have seen happen is the fruition of this book. These dear friends, Bill, Shari, Quinn, Kathy, Phil, Rosie, Menno, Rica, Lee, and

Carla, along with Dan and I have been praying for this book for two years. It has been their prayers that have kept me moving forward, even when I doubted myself.

But what probably blesses me the most is what happens during the time between our gatherings. This group doesn't just come together for an evening every two weeks and then walk out and forget everything until the next meeting rolls around. We keep lifting each other up in prayer, taking everyone's requests to our Father in heaven. Our group knows that whenever they have a need, all they have to do is make a phone call or send out a text or e-mail, and they immediately have eleven other people praying with them.

I remember one night when I shared with them that our grandson was ill and asked if they would be praying for him. Not only did they pray, but they contacted me in the days that followed to find out how he was doing. That, my friend, is being "Jesus with skin on." That is really caring about those things that concern me and then not just saying they will pray, but actually doing it. They are teaching me, by their example, what it really means to be in the family of God.

I hear people say sometimes that there just isn't anything they can do for God. They say they are too old or too young or too busy or not gifted enough or too uneducated. I beg to differ with them because everyone can pray. God doesn't care how lofty your words sound or whether you speak in proper English. God sees your heart and He loves to hear you, His child, lift the requests of others up to Him. Not only does that bless Him, but it also really blesses those you lift up. It shows them that you care enough to go to the Father on their behalf.

Another thing I am learning is that when you lift others up in prayer, you begin thinking less about your own problems. It's easy to get caught up in our daily grind. We can easily find ourselves wallowing in those things that are wrong in our lives and quickly become pretty depressed. But when we can get our eyes off ourselves and onto the lives of those around us, suddenly our spirit is lifted and we become thankful instead of critical or despondent.

If you aren't a member of a small group of believers, I highly recommend that you seek one out. If your life is fairly chaotic, having brothers and sisters in Christ whom you can "do life with" is a wonderful way to regain some sanity. I believe you will soon be blessed as you begin doing this, and doubly blessed as you have the opportunity to share life with them. Believe me when I say that it's a win-win situation!

My Jesus Prayer

> *Jesus, what a blessing it is to have a circle of friends who make me want to be a better follower of You. May those who don't have this blessing begin to seek out those with whom You want them to share their life. What a wonderful way this is to love each other as You have commanded.*

DAY 85
Off The Grid

I wait quietly before God, for my victory comes from him (Psalm 62:1).

Well, I survived. I had made the decision to attend a spiritual retreat where I had to go off the grid for a few days. No phone, no watch, and no computer. Anyone who knows me well understands that it would be no easy task for me. I love to keep in contact with friends and family through texts, calls, and e-mails, and I love to use my computer to write; so having to go three-and-a-half days without the ability to do any of those things made me twitch a little bit.

One of the rules of this retreat was that you were not to have anything with you that could be a distraction. As we all know, it is common that whenever you are with another person or a group of people, texts are pinging, phones are ringing, and many are searching the Internet. So it made sense to remove anything to do with social media.

I was sure that I would miss my phone the most, so I was surprised when that wasn't the case. What did I really miss? Not having my watch on my wrist! More than anything, it drove me nuts. Not having a clue about the time made me just a little stir crazy at times. I never learned how to tell time by the position of the sun, and I couldn't tell the time by how hungry I was because I just might have eaten quite a bit of candy between meals. As a result, I never really suffered from hunger.

Those few days made me realize how often I look at my watch in a day's time. Over and over again I caught myself looking at my wrist, only to see the pale, untanned skin where my watch usually resided. Each time I glanced down and realized nothing was there reminded me of why I was at this retreat.

Those days helped me realize how important it was to remove ourselves periodically from the chaos around us. We live in a world where the tyranny of the urgent often dictates what we do next, and that often leads us to feel somewhat chained to the clock. We need to get this job done by a certain time, run this child to the next practice, get this meal fixed so that another child can get to a game, this report done to share with the finance board at church, and this shower taken quickly so we can go to bed, and then do it all over again the next day. All the while, our texts are piling up, our phone is ringing, and our clocks just keep ticking away the minutes.

It's no wonder so many people have high blood pressure and ulcers. It's no wonder families are falling apart because everyone is going in a thousand different directions. It's no wonder so many have lost their focus and become too busy to spend time with their Savior.

My prayer is that if you find yourself at the same place that I was when I left on this retreat, these words will bring healing to your tired soul. Jesus is waiting for you, and all you have to do is meet Him. I can't begin to tell you how much He longs to spend time with you and how badly He wants to carry your burdens for you.

Don't ever forget that He desperately loves you, and so do I.

My Jesus Prayer

Jesus, I know how important it is to spend time with You. Help me to make it a priority so that the pressures of this world will not control me.

DAY 86
Life Happens

You will keep in perfect peace all who trust in you, all whose thoughts are fixed on you! (Isaiah 26:3).

From the mountaintop to the valley" is the phrase one often hears used to describe it. Something occurs in your life that is amazing, maybe even miraculous and you have what they call a "mountaintop experience." Oftentimes it is a result of a spiritual experience in a meeting or a retreat where you felt the Holy Spirit working in a very powerful way. Your heart is full of praise and overflowing with joy. Your spirit and emotions are flying high and you can attest to the fact that your God is alive and well and still changing lives. You are ready to face the world and nothing will ever dampen your spirits again.

Then you come home. You return to a job that you hate, the kids get sick and you are emptying buckets and taking temperatures, and then your spouse is stepping on your last nerve. Even the dog is irritating you. Unfortunately, it doesn't take you long to realize that you are no longer on the mountaintop. You feel like you have plummeted into the valley of despair. How in the world can you go from feeling like you have the world by the tail to feeling like God is nowhere to be found? Where did you go wrong?

Let me tell you, my friend, that you didn't go wrong; you are just proving that life happens. We live in a fallen world and God never promised that we would always be on the mountaintop. Life is made up of detours and unexpected hiccups, and sometimes it just isn't pretty.

I shared yesterday that I had attended a weekend retreat that was inspiring. I saw God work during those days in ways that amazed me and I came home feeling like I could take on the world. My spirit was refreshed, my relationship with Christ was strengthened, and I felt peace like I hadn't felt for a long time.

Then life happened. My dad became ill and I had to rush him to the ER. He was admitted to the hospital for sixteen days! Our furnace quit working and we were told that it couldn't be fixed so we had to purchase a new one. Then, my dear friend's husband lost his battle with cancer and went home to be with the Lord at the age of sixty-two. Thanksgiving was quickly approaching, and because of the unexpected detours of those past weeks I was nowhere near ready to have thirty-three people in my home on that Thursday.

I don't know about you, but when I'm in the middle of everyday life I sometimes struggle to see the mountaintop because I'm face down in the valley. My head is so buried in the troubles swirling around me that I forget to turn over and look up. You see, whether we are in the valley or on the mountaintop, we can look up at the same heavens, but we have to be intentional about looking upward. Keeping our eyes focused on the One who knows our today and our tomorrow can make a huge difference on how we respond when life happens.

I was determined to not let the events of those past weeks deter me from shouting from the valley that our God is alive and well. I told my husband that God knew every detail of my days way before I did and I was going to let Him do the worrying. I decided that instead of just *saying* that I was thankful on that Thanksgiving, I was going to do my best to *show* Him how thankful I was by trusting Him to orchestrate my steps. If He can turn water into wine, He could surely help me get meat on the table for those whom we couldn't wait to welcome into our home. He alone was worthy to be praised, and I planned to do just that, whether I was in the valley or on the mountaintop!

As you go through your day, I challenge you to join me in showing God how thankful you are that He is a God that can be trusted even when life happens!

My Jesus Prayer

Jesus, I know that when I feel overwhelmed, it isn't You who has moved, it is me. Help me to remember to look up to You, knowing that You are ready and willing to fill me with Your peace even when life happens.

ASK ME ABOUT MY JESUS

DAY 87
'Tis The Season

For just as the heavens are higher than the earth, so my ways are higher than your ways and my thoughts higher than your thoughts (Isaiah 55:9).

It's common to hear the phrase *'tis the season* during December. 'Tis the season for celebrating Christ's birth. 'Tis the season for shopping. 'Tis the season for gift giving. 'Tis the season for family gatherings. 'Tis the season for eating too much, so 'tis the season for elastic-waist pants.

Christmas isn't the only time though when we use this phrase. When our children were young, I remember saying 'tis the season for sleepless nights, toys everywhere, and absolutely no privacy. As they grew, the season changed to school projects, first dates, and college selections. Then the season changed to an empty nest, weddings, and returned privacy. But now, in my fifties, 'tis the season for helping with grandchildren, helping our parents, and losing some of our privacy again.

As I look back on my life, I realize that there have been seasons of my life when I just existed. I just endured the day-to-day grind of living, waiting for the next season to begin. Instead of embracing how God had placed me and being open and available to learn whatever He had to teach me during those days, I squirmed and gritted my teeth while I begged Him to hurry it along. As a result, the memories aren't filled with times of growth and precious moments with my Jesus.

I think it is important to remember that wherever we find ourselves today, 'tis the season. In other words, whatever stage of life we are in, it will only last for a relatively short span of time. Our circumstances usually change and those seasons become memories. The kind of memories we have depends on the attitude we displayed during our season. If we complained and grumbled, then our memories will not be pleasant and might be filled with regret. But if we chose to have joy in wherever God placed us, our memories will continue to give us more joy and contentment.

I don't know what season you find yourself in today. You may be single and wondering if God will ever bring you a soul mate. You may be married and wondering if God will ever bless you with children. You may have children, but wonder if you will ever make it through the toddler stage. Your children may be teenagers and you are wondering if you will survive the constant hormone changes. You may have just entered the empty nest season and you wonder how you will find joy in such a quiet home. Or, you may be in my season, where grandchildren often fill your home with noise and laughter and at the same time you are helping to care for your elderly parents who need your "parenting" touch.

All seasons have challenges. All seasons have pain. All seasons have joy. All seasons can be lived for God's glory. But how we look back on that season will depend on our attitude while we are in that time frame.

We are promised that God *will* see us through each day, each week, each month, and each year. He doesn't promise that each day will end exactly the way we had planned, but if we submit to Him, He promises that each season will end according to *His* perfect plan. That should give us hope and peace and the strength needed for the next twenty-four hours. Never forget: *'Tis the Season for Him* to work in a mighty way wherever He has placed you today.

My Jesus Prayer

> *Jesus, wherever I find myself today, help me to remember that Your plan is always perfect. In this season, I can find joy, peace, and strength if I stay focused on You.*

ASK ME ABOUT MY JESUS

DAY 88
Life's Videos

I prayed to the Lord, and he answered me. He freed me from all my fears (Psalm 34:4).

We had many, many VHS tapes that we had recorded over the years. Christmases, birthdays, family gatherings, and even a pretzel-making day had all been captured on video to remind us of those memory-making days as our children were being raised.

My husband decided to take on the huge project of transferring all of those tapes onto our computer. Knowing that VHS tapes can sometimes break as they age, he wanted to make sure that their contents were preserved for many years to come. There was no way to recreate all of those priceless moments, so even though it would take him hours to transfer them, it would be well worth the trouble.

He had all of his equipment set up in my library, so it was fun to check out my computer screen when I entered that room to see which tape he was currently transferring. Seeing and hearing our children when they were young just warmed my heart. I know those were exhausting days that sometimes seemed as though they would never end, but just as I was warned then by older more experienced moms, it now seems like I blinked and they were all grown up.

One thing that struck me in those tapes was that many of the scenes looked like they were staged for a television program. Most of the people being videoed were on their best behavior, knowing that the tape was rolling. Not once did I tell my husband, "Quick! Get the video camera and film me while I lose my temper with the kids." The reason is that I don't want to remember those times when I failed as a mom, a wife, a sister, or a daughter. And I surely don't want those times recorded for everyone else to watch over and over.

But then, I don't need a recording to remind me of my past failures. Many of them are permanently cemented in my brain and it doesn't take much to bring them into my thoughts. Oftentimes those memories creep back in when I'm getting ready to do something positive that the Lord is leading me to do. All of a sudden…*wham*…my mind goes back in time and those past shortcomings make me question whether I am capable or worthy to do His work now. Even those instances when I knew I was wrong and asked the Lord to forgive me, still come back to cause an unsettled spirit as I struggle to forgive myself.

Unfortunately, I don't think I'm alone in this. I have talked to many others that can relate to this scenario. Many of us dwell on the past and in doing so, we become stagnant in our relationship with Christ and fail to move forward. Satan knows that as long as he can keep us reliving our failures over and over, he doesn't have to worry about us doing the Lord's will today.

There are also times when it isn't our past shortcomings that we dwell on, but someone else's. I'm confident that all of us have, at some point, been deeply hurt by a friend, a family member, or even a stranger, and forgiving that person seems impossible. As a result, we can easily dwell on the pain from that moment and allow it to make us feel like we are on a stationary bike, exerting a lot of emotion but going nowhere.

If we neglect to deal with our past, it can make us fear the future and we can be overwhelmed with the "what-ifs" of life. *What if* we say or do the wrong thing and let someone else down? *What if* we take a chance and reach out to someone and that person hurts us in return? *What if* we step way out of our comfort zone and fall flat on our face and we feel like a total failure?

It is at these moments when we need to remember that there is nothing from our past that the Lord cannot forgive or that can stop Him from loving us. Nor is there any pain from our past that He cannot heal. There is also nothing in our future that He cannot handle.

If you feel you are in a "holding pattern" right now, I urge you to think about this: If someone watches a video ten years from now of your day today, what do you want them to see? Do you want them to see you scared, discouraged, and overwhelmed with your past or do you want them to see you living a life that is prayer-driven and God-directed? Living a life that is fueled with His Spirit is a life that will have an impact on others for many years to come. Who knows? Your choices today just might lead to the most exciting days in life ever because our times are never boring when He is in control!

My Jesus Prayer

> *Jesus, when others look back on my life, I want them to see me as someone who was prayer-driven and God-directed. I want my life to have had an impact on eternity, so help me today to make sure and tell those I see about my Jesus.*

LUANN GERIG FULTON

DAY 89

Taming My Unibrow

Finally, I confessed all my sins to you and stopped trying to hide my guilt. I said to myself, "I will confess my rebellion to the Lord." (Psalm 32:5).

Our oldest daughter, Erica, lives in North Carolina. She loves living in this beautiful state, but we sure miss not having her close to us, so it is always a treat to be able to spend time with her.

Erica enjoys hiking on Saturday mornings in the state park close to her home, so we were thrilled to be able to do that with her on one of our visits. It was a warm day in the 90s, but knowing that a little sweat never hurt anyone, we climbed in our truck and headed for the trail. Afterward we took showers and then headed to lunch for good food and great conversation.

We had already decided what would be on our agenda following lunch. We knew we would do something that I do every time I visit Erica. It is something that I have never done at home, but always make a point to get accomplished when I'm in North Carolina. Erica directed us to an area business where I got my eyebrows threaded.

In case you don't know what eyebrow threading is, a thin thread is doubled, and then twisted. It is then rolled over areas of unwanted hair, plucking the hair at the follicle level. Unlike tweezing, where single hairs are pulled out one at a time, threading can remove short lines of hair. There are lots of people who think this is a sadistic form of torture, but I enjoy it. I have been "blessed" with very heavy eyebrows and it takes time and effort to keep them from becoming a unibrow. The problem is that I don't often take the time to keep them under control and so it makes me feel so good when I can get them cleaned up and shaped in just a few minutes. The thing is that even though it seems like it at times, my eyebrows don't get out of control overnight. It happens gradually, one hair at a time. If I would just make sure and take care of the unwanted strands as they appeared, it wouldn't be such a major chore to get them shaped. Unfortunately, I tend to ignore the signs until it's a major task to get them shaped and contoured.

This is also what happens when sin begins to creep into my life. I know I've shared before during these ninety days how easily this can happen. It usually doesn't occur overnight or show itself in a grand fashion. It usually presents itself in small ways in the beginning and it's easy to overlook it and think it isn't a big deal. The problem with that is that those small "insignificant" sins begin to add up, and before I know it, sin has taken over and it takes a much bigger effort on my part to get things cleaned up. God is able and willing to forgive me no matter what I've done, but then I have to deal with the consequences of those things that I have allowed to creep in that have gone against His plan for my life.

Hopefully you and I have been more intentional over the last three months to make sure that we deal with sin as soon as it rears its ugly head, instead of allowing it to slowly infiltrate our lives. Just as it feels good when our outward appearance is under control, it feels even better when our heart is clean and in tune with God's will. But we know we have to be willing to take the time each and every day to follow His leading and make the choices He would want us to make. By doing that, our lives will be much easier in the days and weeks to come because we won't have to clean up the consequences of our neglect.

My Jesus Prayer

Jesus, we so desperately want to be the disciples that You intend us to be. Help us deal with any sin as soon as it makes an appearance so that we will reflect You to those we meet. We know that only then will they want to hear about our Jesus.

DAY 90
A Glimpse Of Heaven

But if we confess our sins to him, he is faithful and just to forgive us our sins and to cleanse us from all wickedness (1 John 1:9).

As we wrap up our ninety days together, I want to share an experience in my life that left me changed. It was a week that I will never forget. I sat in the ICU with a family as they waited for their loved one to take her last breath here on earth, and her first breath in eternity. The next day, I received word that a dear friend of mine was diagnosed with stage four cancer. To say the week was an emotional one for me is an understatement.

Those events reminded me again that this life we live is just a brief segment of time in light of eternity. No matter how long any of us are given on this earth, that number of days doesn't hold a candle to being in eternity forever. I'm afraid many of us get so wrapped up with our day-to-day responsibilities that we fail to remember that this world is not our home, that we are just passing through on our way to living forever either in heaven or in hell. You might think that I am too blunt, but it's time that we realize that our decision to accept Jesus or not will determine where we will spend eternity.

Many believe they will be in heaven because they lived a good life; they never intentionally hurt anyone or did anything that would have been considered bad. Or they might be thinking they will be in heaven on the shirttails of their parents. Their parents were Christians, so that makes them Christians too. The truth is that your parents can't "get you in"; in the same way, being the member of a church can't earn your way to heaven either. The only way to make sure that you will spend your forever and forever in heaven is to personally accept Jesus Christ as your Lord and Savior.

ASK ME ABOUT MY JESUS

At the other end of the emotional spectrum of that week, we had all of our children sitting around our table Saturday evening. Since our children live in different locations, this is a rarity for us, and it brought great joy to me. A friend of mine texted me while we were together and I told her that all of our family was here and she said, "That's heaven for you and Dan." She said exactly what I had already been thinking. The evening was just a taste of what heaven must be like—fellowshipping with those whom we dearly love, forgetting the cares of this world while enjoying each other's company. As the evening ended, I had the thought that if I had just experienced a teeny-tiny glimpse of heaven, I sure didn't want to miss the real thing.

As we end our time together, I feel led to ask you again: Are you ready? None of us are guaranteed tomorrow and in an instant we can be facing eternity. Will yours be spent in heaven? I can't tell you how much I hope your answer is yes. If you aren't sure, don't delay. Ask to have your sins forgiven and for Jesus Christ to live in your heart. It is the most critical decision you will ever make.

I just can't imagine what it will be like to finally see my Jesus face-to-face and to fellowship around His table. Believe me when I say that if that Saturday night with my children was a minuscule glimpse of heaven, you surely don't want to miss it. I want to do everything I can to make sure there is place set for you too, but it has to be your decision. Please don't delay. If you need someone to talk with, feel free to contact me. I'm always available for you to ask me about *my* Jesus.

My Jesus Prayer

Jesus, thank You for loving me enough to die for my sins so that I can spend eternity with You. Please help me let others see You in me, so that I can tell them how much You mean to me.

LuAnn would love to hear from you. You may contact her with questions, comments, or to schedule her for speaking engagements on her website at: www.luannfulton.com. You can also follow her blog at theimageseeker.blogspot.com and contact her by e-mail at luannfulton@gmail.com.

5 FOLD MEDiA

We are a Christian-based publishing company that was founded in 2009. Our primary focus has been to establish authors.

"5 Fold Media was the launching partner that I needed to bring *The Transformed Life* into reality. This team worked diligently and with integrity to help me bring my words and vision into manifestation through a book that I am proud of and continues to help people and churches around the world. None of this would have been possible without the partnership and education I received from 5 Fold Media."

- Pastor John Carter, Lead Pastor of Abundant Life Christian Center, Syracuse, NY, Author and Fox News Contributor

*The Transformed Life is foreworded by Pastor A.R. Bernard, received endorsements from best-selling authors Phil Cooke, Rick Renner, and Tony Cooke, and has been featured on television shows such as TBN and local networks.

5 Fold Media
315.570.3333 | 5701 E. Circle Dr. #338, Cicero, NY 13039
manuscript@5foldmedia.com

Find us on Facebook, Twitter, and YouTube.

Discover more at www.5FoldMedia.com.